NEIL SIMON began his writing career in television, writing for *The Phil Silvers Show* and Sid Caesar's *Your Show of Shows*. His first play was *Come Blow Your Horn*, followed by the musical *Little Me*. Since 1960, a New York season without a Neil Simon comedy or musical has been a rare one. His plays include *Barefoot in the Park*, *The Odd Couple*, *Sweet Charity*, *The Star-Spangled Girl*, *Plaza Suite*, *Last of the Red Hot Lovers*, *Promises, Promises*, *The Gingerbread Lady*, *The Prisoner of Second Avenue*, *The Sunshine Boys*, *The Good Doctor*, *God's Favorite*, *California Suite*, *Chapter Two*, *They're Playing Our Song*, *I Ought to Be in Pictures*, *Fools*, *Brighton Beach Memoirs*, *Biloxi Blues* (which won the Tony Award for Best Play), *Broadway Bound*, *Rumors*, and *Jake's Women*. He has adapted nearly all of them for the screen. His other screenplays include *After the Fox*, *The Out-of-Towners*, *The Heartbreak Kid*, *Murder by Death*, *The Goodbye Girl*, *The Cheap Detective*, *Seems Like Old Times*, *Only When I Laugh*, and *Max Dugan Returns*. He received the Tony Award and the Pulitzer Prize in 1991 for *Lost in Yonkers*. He is married to Diane Lander and has three daughters, Ellen, Nancy, and Bryn.

Tone — relationship butn author + audience

attitude - relationship between author and subject

Grandma sets the tone - she is rigid - can't adjust

doesn't want to show vulnerability

LOST IN YONKERS

BY

Neil Simon

A PLUME BOOK

PLUME
Published by the Penguin Group
Penguin Books USA Inc., 375 Hudson Street, New York, New York 10014, U.S.A.
Penguin Books Ltd, 27 Wrights Lane, London W8 5TZ, England
Penguin Books Australia Ltd, Ringwood, Victoria, Australia
Penguin Books Canada Ltd, 10 Alcorn Avenue, Toronto, Ontario, Canada M4V 3B2
Penguin Books (N.Z.) Ltd, 182-190 Wairau Road, Auckland 10, New Zealand

Penguin Books Ltd, Registered Offices: Harmondsworth, Middlesex, England

Published by Plume, an imprint of New American Library,
a division of Penguin Books USA Inc. This is an authorized reprint of a hardcover
edition published by Random House, Inc., and simultaneously published in Canada
by Random House of Canada, Ltd.

First Plume Printing, January, 1993
10 9 8

 REGISTERED TRADEMARK—MARCA REGISTRADA

LIBRARY OF CONGRESS CATALOGING-IN-PUBLICATION DATA
Simon, Neil.
    Lost in Yonkers / by Neil Simon.
        p.   cm.
    ISBN 0-452-26883-4
    I. Title.
    [PS3537.I663L67   1993]
    812'.54—dc20   92-29111
                                                       CIP

Printed in the United States of America

FOR DIANE
WITH LOVE

Lost in Yonkers by Neil Simon was first presented by Emanuel Azenberg at the Stevens Center for the Performing Arts in Winston-Salem, North Carolina, on December 31, 1990, and subsequently opened in New York City on February 21, 1991, with the following cast:

JAY	Jamie Marsh
ARTY	Danny Gerard
EDDIE	Mark Blum
BELLA	Mercedes Ruehl
GRANDMA KURNITZ	Irene Worth
LOUIE	Kevin Spacey
GERT	Lauren Klein

Gene Saks was the director. The scenery and costumes were designed by Santo Loquasto, the lighting by Tharon Musser, the sound by Tom Morse, and Peter Lawrence was the production supervisor.

Act One

Yonkers, New York, 1942.

We are in an apartment that sits just above "Kurnitz's Kandy Store." . . . *It consists of a living room, dining room, small kitchen, one bathroom, and two bedrooms. The entrance door leads from downstairs directly to the candy store.*

It's about six-thirty in the evening on a hot, sultry day in August. It's still quite light outside. A fan blows in the living room.

Two young boys are in the living room. One, ARTHUR KURNITZ, *about thirteen and a half, sits on an old armchair, looking apprehensive. He is wearing an old woolen suit, his only one, with knickered pants, a shirt, tie, long socks, and brown shoes.*

The other boy is his brother, JAY KURNITZ, *not quite sixteen. He sits on the sofa, in a suit as well, but with long pants, shirt, tie, and shiny black shoes. He looks more sullen and angry than apprehensive.*

ARTY *keeps wiping his sweaty brow with his handkerchief.*

JAY   I hate coming here, don't you?

ARTY *(In front of fan)*   It's hot. I'm so hot.

JAY   I'd hate coming here if I was cool. Pop doesn't even like to come and it's his own mother . . . I was so afraid of her when I was a kid. She'd come out of that door with a limp and a cane and look like she was going to kill you. When I was five, I drew a picture of her and called it "Frankenstein's Grandma."

ARTY   Did she ever see it?

3

JAY   If she did, you'd be an only child today. Pop said she could swing her cane so fast, she could have been one of the greatest golfers in the world.

ARTY   All I remember was, I hated kissing her. It felt like putting your lips on a wrinkled ice cube.

JAY   Yeah, she's cold alright. She was the only one at Mom's funeral who didn't cry . . . I wonder what Pop's talking to her so long for.

ARTY   Because she's deaf in one ear, isn't she?

JAY   Yeah . . . Did you ever notice there's something wrong with *everyone* on Pop's side of the family? Mom used to tell me that.

ARTY   She didn't tell me. Like who?

JAY   Like all of them. Like Aunt Bella . . . She's a little— *(Points to his head)*—you know—closed for repairs.

ARTY   I don't care. I like her. Nicer than "hot house" Grandma.

JAY   I didn't say she wasn't nice. But she's got marbles rolling around up there . . . Mom said she got that way because when she was a kid, Grandma kept hitting her in the head every time she did something stupid . . . which only made her stupider.

ARTY   *(He lies down on the floor, in front of the sofa)* She wasn't stupid at making great ice cream sodas.

JAY Hooray! Wonderful! She's thirty-five years old and she can make ice cream sodas. They don't give you a high school diploma for getting the cherry on top of the whipped cream.

ARTY She went to high school?

JAY A little. She missed the first year because she couldn't find it.

(*The bedroom door opens. Their father,* EDDIE KUR-NITZ, *about forty-one, steps out into the room. He wears a suit and tie and seems hot and nervous. He wipes his brow with a hanky*)

EDDIE You kids alright?

JAY Yeah, Pop. Fine.

EDDIE I'll be through talking to Grandma in a few minutes. (*To* ARTY) What are you lying on the floor? Don't do that, Arty. You'll crease your pants. You want Grandma to see you with creased pants?

(*He goes back in and closes the door*)

ARTY (*Stands*) What's he want me to do, carry an iron with me?

JAY He's afraid of her the same as Aunt Bella. Like Aunt Bella couldn't count so good, so instead of two scoops of ice cream in a soda, she'd put in three or four. For the same price. And if Grandma saw it, Whacko! Another couple of IQ points gone. (*He picks up a photo from behind the sofa)* Here, look at this. Aunt Gert when she was a kid! See how her head is down? Probably ducking. The old cane was coming at her . . . You don't think Aunt Gert's a little coconuts too?

ARTY   No. She's just sick. She's got bad lungs or something.

JAY   Bad lungs, my eye. She can't talk right. She says the first half of a sentence breathing out and the second half sucking in. You've seen it.

ARTY   Do it for me.

JAY   I don't want to.

ARTY   Come on, do it.

JAY   No, I don't want to.

ARTY   Do it!

JAY   *(Imitating* AUNT GERT. *He breathes out)* "Oh, hello, Jay, how are you? And how is your father? And— *(Then talks as he sucks in breath)*—how is your little brother, Arty?"

ARTY   *(Laughs)*   I love it! I love when you do that.

JAY   I once saw her try to blow out a candle and halfway there she sucked it back on.

ARTY   You didn't.

JAY With these two eyes. Mom says she talks that way because she was so afraid of Grandma. She never allowed her kids to cry.

ARTY Never?

JAY Never. Well, if you're growing up here like Aunt Gert and you're not allowed to cry, you're going to end up sucking in the last half of your sentences.

(EDDIE *comes back in*)

EDDIE Grandma's worried about the doilies. Don't lean your head back on the doilies. It gets grease on them. She just had them laundered.

(He goes back in)

ARTY *(To* JAY*)* You mean only people who just had a shampoo can sit here?

JAY And what about Uncle Louie? You know what *he* is, don't you?

ARTY Yeah. A gangster. You believe that?

JAY You bet. They say he's some big mobster's henchman.

ARTY You mean he's got a bad back?

JAY Not a hunchback. A *henchman!* . . . And real tough. He's a bagman.

ARTY   What do you mean, a bagman? He puts people in bags?

JAY   Not people. Money. *Hot* money. He collects bags of it from one guy and delivers it to the mob . . . (ARTY *rises and crosses to the window*) Listen, I'm not going to tell you any more because he could walk right in on us. They say he comes back here to sleep every once in a while.

ARTY (*Looking out the window*)   Hey! There's Aunt Bella . . .

JAY   Is she coming up?

ARTY   No. She's walking past the house.

JAY   I'll bet she's lost again. (*He looks out the window, then calls down*) Aunt Bella? . . . Hi! . . . It's Jay and Arty . . . Up here. (*He waves to her*) That's right. Up here . . . Here she comes. (*They walk away from the window*) She ought to wear a compass or something.

(*The bedroom door opens.* EDDIE *comes out again*)

EDDIE   Will you keep your voices down. Grandma said, "What are they yelling for?"

JAY   We were calling down to Aunt Bella. She's on her way up.

ARTY   Can I take my jacket off?

EDDIE   After Grandma sees you. And no ice cream sodas from Aunt Bella. Even if she asks you. I don't want to get Grandma upset now. Fix the doilies.

JAY   Is she alright?

EDDIE   Her back is bothering her. When Aunt Bella comes in, tell her Momma wants a back rub . . . Comb your hair, Arty, and don't make a mess.

> (EDDIE *goes back in. We hear a knock on the front door*)

BELLA   *(Offstage)* Jay? Arty? It's me. Aunt Bella. Can I come in?

JAY   Guess who forgot how to open a door? . . .

> (JAY *opens the door.* BELLA KURNITZ, *in her mid-thirties, stands there. Although she's a mess at dressing—nothing matches at all—she is neat and sweet and pretty, if looking a little older than her age. She's as warm and congenial as she is emotionally arrested*)

BELLA   *(Smiles)*   I forgot my key.

JAY   How'd you get in downstairs?

BELLA   I used my spare key. I'm glad you called me. I walked right by the house, didn't I? Sometimes I daydream so much, I think I should carry an alarm clock . . . Oh, God, I'm so happy to see you. Arty! Jay! My two favorite cousins.

JAY   Aren't we your nephews?

BELLA   Of course you are. My cousins, my nephews, my boys. Come here, give your Aunt Bella a kiss. *(She puts down her purse, pulls* JAY *and* ARTY *into her arms, and kisses them both)* Let me look at you. You both got so much bigger. You're growing up so fast, it almost makes me cry . . . Where's your father? I haven't seen your father in so long . . . *(She calls out)* Eddie! It's Bella . . . Is he here?

ARTY   He's in there, talking to Grandma.

BELLA   *(Suddenly nervous)*   Oh, I'd better not disturb them . . . Did she ask for me?

JAY   Pop said her back was hurting. She wanted you to give her a back rub when you came in?

BELLA   Oh. Did you tell her I was here?

JAY   No. You just came in.

BELLA   Did you tell her where I went?

JAY   We didn't know where you went.

BELLA   Well, let's not tell her I'm here yet. Then we won't be able to visit. *(She takes off her sweater)* Oh, you're both getting so handsome.

JAY   Thank you.

ARTY   Thank you, Aunt Bella.

BELLA   I bet I look much older to you two. Do I? The truth. Tell me.

JAY   I don't think so.

ARTY No.

BELLA I was hoping you'd say that. I'm thirty-five. And I don't even look it, do I?

JAY No.

ARTY Not to me.

BELLA And how old are you boys now? About twenty?

ARTY I'm thirteen and a half.

JAY I'm fifteen and a half.

BELLA Well, that adds up to about thirty-five. So we could be brother and sisters. Isn't that wonderful?

JAY Yeah.

BELLA Yeah . . . I just got back from the movies. I had the most wonderful time. I wish I knew you were here, we all could have gone.

JAY What did you see?

BELLA I don't know. I couldn't find the theater I was looking for, so I went to the one I found. But it was better than the picture I wanted to see. It was with Bette Davis and George Brent . . . Maybe we could all go again next week, if I can find the wrong theater again.

ARTY Sure. I'd love to.

JAY   Except we won't be here next week. We're going to the Yankee game with Pop.

BELLA   Oh, well, you do that. Boys like baseball much better than love stories . . . Why don't you take your jackets off, you two? Look at you both perspiring.

ARTY   We're fine. We're cool in here with the fan.

BELLA   That fan doesn't cool anything off. It just makes the hot air go faster . . . They had air-conditioning at the movie house. I was actually cold. I felt so happy for the actors to be in an air-conditioned theater.

JAY *(He looks at* ARTY, *then at* BELLA*)*   I don't think the actors feel it. They're just pictures on the screen.

BELLA   Well, I know that, silly. I meant they'd be happy to know that people who were watching their movies were nice and cool so we enjoyed the movie better.

JAY   Oh. Right. I bet they would.

BELLA   I bet I know what would make you two cool in a second. How about a big ice cream soda deluxe? With everything in it? Look at your faces lighting up. Come on. I'll make it for you downstairs.

JAY   I think we have to wait here. Pop'll be out in a second and he wants us to see Grandma.

BELLA   Well, I'll bring them up here. That's no trouble. What kind? Chocolate? Vanilla? Butter Pecan? What's your favorite, Arty?

ARTY   All of them.

BELLA   I can make that. With three different kinds of ice cream. I used to make one with *four* different kinds. They were selling like crazy, but we lost a fortune . . . How long ago did she ask for me?

JAY   Grandma? A couple of minutes ago.

BELLA   Did you tell her I was here?

JAY   No, we told Pop we saw you from the window. But maybe he didn't say anything to her.

BELLA   It doesn't make any difference. She heard my footsteps coming up the stairs.

ARTY   How? Isn't she partly deaf?

BELLA   Oh, sure. But the other part hears perfectly . . . What about a small sundae? Chocolate ice cream with hot-fudge sauce and some whipped cream and chopped walnuts? Are you going to say no to that, Arthur? I bet you can't. Say no. Let me hear you.

ARTY *(He looks at* JAY*)*   It sounds like just a small one.

JAY *(To* BELLA*)*   He can't. We're having dinner soon. It's just that Pop told us to wait.

BELLA   Oh, your father. He never takes anything from anybody. I couldn't even give your mother a cup of coffee . . . Did you know that? . . . Where is she, anyway?

(JAY *looks confused*)

JAY   She's dead. Mom is dead.

BELLA *(She looks confused a moment)*   Yes. I know . . . I mean where is she buried?

JAY   At Mount Israel Cemetery in the Bronx. You were at the funeral. Remember?

BELLA   You mean the first time?

JAY   What do you mean, the first time?

BELLA   When I came in the car. Not the bus.

ARTY   The bus?

BELLA *(Thinks . . .)*   No. No. I'm thinking of someone else. Sometimes my mind wanders. The kids in school used to say, "Hey, Bella. Lost and Found called and said, 'Come get your brains.' " . . . *(She laughs)* . . . but I didn't think that was funny. *(The boys nod)* I bet you miss Mom a lot, don't you? Don't you, Arty?

ARTY   Yeah. A lot.

BELLA   She was a lot like your father. Very independent. Stuck to her own family mostly. *(She lowers her voice)* She didn't get along too well with your grandmother. Nobody does. My sister, Gert, was once engaged to a man. She brought him over to meet Grandma. The next day he moved to Boston.

JAY   That's too bad.

BELLA   Don't tell Grandma I said that.

ARTY   I won't.

BELLA   What?

ARTY   I won't.

BELLA   You're both so shy. I used to be shy. Grandma didn't like me to talk too much . . . I had a lot of friends, but I didn't talk to them . . . It's a shame your mother couldn't have had more children . . . She didn't, did she?

JAY   No.

BELLA   No . . . Because it would be easier for you now that she's gone. Big families are important when you have trouble in your life. We were a big family . . . Me and your father and Louie and Gert . . . That was before Rose and Aaron died . . . Rose was just a baby but Aaron was almost twelve so I didn't know Rose as well as Aaron . . . You never knew them, did you?

JAY   I don't think we were born yet.

BELLA   No. I don't think so . . . My father died before I was born. But I wasn't sad about that.

JAY   That's good.

BELLA   Because I loved him so much. Did you know you could love somebody who died before you were born?

JAY   I guess so.

BELLA   Because I knew he would have taken care of me
. . . Like your father takes care of you. You know what
I mean?

JAY   I think so.

BELLA   So what about that sundae? It's going to sit down
there melting on the counter if I make it and you don't
eat it . . . Last time I'm asking, Arthur. Yes or no?

ARTY   I'd . . . I'd like to . . . *(He looks at* JAY *who shakes
his head "No")* . . . Maybe later.

BELLA   *(Snaps coldly, angrily)*   NO! NOT LATER!!
IT'S TOO LATE NOW!!! . . . I'm not asking you
again. You hurt my feelings, the both of you. You tell
your father to teach you better manners before I'm ever
nice to you again . . . I know you miss your mother but
that doesn't mean you can be disrespectful to me
. . . I *always* liked your mother whether she took coffee
from me or not. And you can tell that to your father,
the both of you. You hear me? . . . I'm sick of it.

> *(She goes into the bathroom and slams the door hard.*
> JAY *and* ARTY *just look at each other)*

JAY   You see why I don't like to come here too much?

> *(The bedroom door opens, and a bedraggled* EDDIE
> *comes out and looks around)*

EDDIE   Where's Aunt Bella? I thought I just heard her.

JAY   She's in the bathroom.

EDDIE   I heard the door slam. Did you say anything to upset her?

JAY   Yeah. Everything.

ARTY   Is it time to go yet, Pop?

EDDIE   We'll go when I tell you. You haven't even seen your grandmother. Stop rushing me. You just got here, didn't you?

ARTY   It's okay. Talk as long as you want, Pop.

EDDIE   And then the three of us have to talk. You, me, and Arty. *(He knocks on the bathroom door)* Bella! It's Eddie. Momma wants to see you. It's her back again . . . Bella? *(No answer. To the boys)* Is she alright?

JAY   How do you know when she's alright?

EDDIE   Hey! No remarks about Aunt Bella, you hear me? She loves you boys. Always has. She'd do anything for you two. So just sit there and be quiet. God, my head is splitting.

> *(He goes back into the bedroom and closes the door.*
>
> The bathroom door opens and BELLA *steps out, holding a towel and oil)*

BELLA   Was that your father banging on the door just now?

JAY   Yes.

BELLA Is he angry with me?

JAY With you? No.

BELLA I hope not. Do I look better?

ARTY Better than when?

BELLA Than before. When you said I wasn't looking well.

ARTY I didn't say that.

BELLA Then who said it? . . . Jay?

ARTY Maybe. Did you say it, Jay?

JAY Nobody said anything.

BELLA Oh. I know. It was Grandma. She didn't like the way I looked today. She hates this dress . . . I made it myself.

ARTY Really?

BELLA *(She nods)* It took me almost a year.

JAY . . . Grandma wants you, Aunt Bella.

BELLA Oh, yeah . . . As soon as I finish Momma's rub, I'll start dinner . . . Are you boys hungry?

ARTY I don't know. Jay knows. Tell her, Jay.

JAY I'm not so sure we're staying for dinner.

BELLA Of course you are. You think I'd let you go all the way home without dinner? . . . Are you going to say no to me again, Arty?

ARTY *(Quickly)* I'm not. I'm eating. I'm hungry. No matter what Jay does. I'm eating.

BELLA Well, we're *all* eating. It's Sunday. The family always eats together on Sunday. And you think about what you want for dessert, Arty, because whatever you want is what you're going to get . . . Start thinking now.

ARTY I started! I started! I want a big ice cream soda with a sundae with whipped cream and hot-fudge sauce. Is that okay?

BELLA Sounds perfect to me. And don't give any to Jay. He missed the deadline.

(*She puts her nose up to* JAY *and goes into* GRANDMA's *room*)

ARTY *(To* JAY*)* Don't be mad. I had to say it. I was afraid she was going to strangle me with the towel.

JAY It's up to Pop. We'll see what Pop says.

(ARTY *lies on the sofa. The bedroom door opens.* EDDIE *comes out. He looks strained. He crosses to the open window and takes a deep breath of air*)

EDDIE Jay! Get me a glass of water, please.

JAY Right, Pop.

(He rushes into the kitchen)

EDDIE It must be over a hundred in here. *(He looks at ARTY)* Get your shoes off the sofa, what's wrong with you?

ARTY *(Moves his shoes)* I'm feeling kind of faint.

EDDIE What do you mean, faint? Kids your age don't faint.

ARTY Maybe I'm getting older.

JAY *(He comes in with the glass)* Here you go, Pop. Nice and cool.

EDDIE Don't spill it on the rug. *(He takes the glass and drinks, then puts the glass down)* Alright . . . Time to talk. Sit down, Jay. Next to Arty. *(JAY sits on the sofa next to ARTY. EDDIE sits on the stool. He is thinking about how to start)* I er . . . I wanted to tell you boys—

(And suddenly he breaks and tears come to his eyes. He quickly tries to stifle it. He wipes his eyes. He goes to the window for some air)

ARTY Is anything the matter, Po—

EDDIE It's so damn hot in here, isn't it? . . . So, I just had a talk inside with your grandmother . . . Because I've had a problem . . . When your mother and I had a problem, we always tried to keep it from you boys because we didn't want to worry you . . . The first year she was sick, I never even told you about it . . . Well, you can't keep cancer a secret forever . . . You knew without me telling you, didn't you, Jay?

JAY   Yes, Pop.

EDDIE   I did everything I could. The best doctors, the best hospital I could get into . . . She had a nice room, didn't she? Semiprivate, no wards or anything . . . I paid the nurse extra to put her next to the window. She loved looking at that tree every day . . . It was worth whatever it cost.

JAY   It was a great tree, Pop.

EDDIE   Do you remember how long she was in that hospital? Remember, Arty?

ARTY   A long time.

EDDIE   Almost four months . . . She wanted to go home because of the money but I knew she wouldn't get the same care at home. Even with a private nurse, they don't always show up. And with this war, you're lucky to find one.

JAY   I know, Pop.

EDDIE   We're not rich people, boys. I know that doesn't come as a surprise to you . . . but I'm going to tell you something now I hoped I'd never have to tell you in my life . . . The doctors, the hospital, cost me everything I had . . . And everything I didn't have . . . And finally it cost me everything I was *going* to have . . . I was broke and I went into debt . . . Into hock . . . Only I

didn't have anything left to hock . . . So I went to a man
. . . A Shylock, they call him . . . A loan shark . . . A
moneylender . . . I couldn't go to a bank because they
don't let you put up heartbreak and pain as collateral
. . . You know what collateral is, Arty? . . . If you want
to borrow ten dollars, you have to give them something
to hold that's worth *eleven* dollars . . . That's for their
interest . . . A Shylock doesn't need collateral . . . His
collateral is your desperation . . . So he gives you his
money . . . And he's got a clock. And when you get
your money, the clock starts . . . And what it keeps time
of is your promise . . . If you keep your promise, he
turns off the clock . . . and if not, it keeps ticking
. . . and after a while, your heart starts ticking louder
than his clock . . . This man becomes a cloud that
darkens your life wherever you go . . . Understand
something. This man kept your mother alive . . . It kept
that tree outside her window . . . It was his painkillers
that made her last days bearable . . . And for that I'm
grateful . . . Jay! Remember what I taught you about
taking things from people?

JAY *(He nods)*   Never take because you'll always be obligated.

EDDIE   So you never take for yourself . . . But for someone you love, there comes a time when you have no
choice . . . There's a man in New York I owe a lot of
money to . . . Nine thousand dollars . . . I don't have
nine thousand dollars . . . I could work and save four
more years and I won't have nine thousand dollars
. . . He wants his money this year. To his credit, I'll say
one thing. He sent flowers to the funeral. No extra
charge on my bill . . .

JAY Pop—

EDDIE Let me finish . . . There is no way I can pay this man back . . . So what'll he do? Kill me? . . . Maybe . . . If he kills me, he not only loses his money, it'll probably cost him again for the flowers for *my* funeral . . . Don't look worried. I'm not going to die . . . I wouldn't tell you all this if there wasn't a happy ending . . . I needed a miracle . . . And the miracle happened . . . This country went to war . . . A war between us and the Japanese and the Germans . . . And if my mother didn't come to this country thirty-five years ago, I could have been fighting for the other side . . . Except I don't think they're putting guns in the hands of Jews over there . . . And if I didn't marry your mother and have two children to support, I'd be fighting for this side . . . I'm too old. So neither side needs me and neither side wants me . . . Except the man with the ticking clock . . . Let me tell you something. I love this country. Because they took in the Jews. They took in the Irish, the Italians, and everyone else . . . Remember this. There's a lot of Germans in this country fighting for America, but there are no Americans over there fighting for Germany . . . I hate this war, and God forgive me for saying this, but it's going to save my life . . . There are jobs I can get now that I could never get before . . . And I got a job . . . I'm working for a company that sells scrap iron . . . I thought you threw scrap iron away. Now they're building ships with it . . . Without even the slightest idea of what I'm doing, I can make that nine thousand dollars in less than a year . . .

JAY That's great, Pop.

EDDIE   Don't say it till I finish . . . The factories that I would sell to are in the South . . . Georgia, Kentucky, Louisiana, Texas, even New Mexico. Places that I never thought I'd see in my lifetime . . . I'd be gone about ten months . . . Living in trains, buses, hotels, any place I can find a room . . . We'd be free and clear and back together again in less than a year . . . Okay? . . . So now comes the question, where do you two live while I'm gone?

(There is a deafening silence as JAY *and* ARTY *turn and look at each other)*

ARTY *(Wiping his brow)*   . . . God, it's so hot in here.

JAY   Please, Pop, don't make us live here . . . That's what you're thinking, isn't it?

EDDIE   I have no choice, Jay. I don't know where else to turn.

JAY *(To* EDDIE*)*   Why can't we stay where we are?

EDDIE   I gave the apartment up. I told the landlady yesterday.

ARTY *(Astonished)*   You gave it up?

EDDIE   She raised the rent. *Every*body's looking to make money out of this war. And the truth is, by the end of the year, it'll be eleven thousand. While I'm away, the clock doesn't stop ticking.

JAY   Grandma wouldn't be happy with us. We're slobs.
We leave everything on the floor. Arty's always breaking things.

ARTY *(To* EDDIE*)*   Remember when I broke the good
water pitcher? And the ink stains on the sofa. All mine!
. . . I'm dangerous, Pop.

EDDIE   Listen to me, both of you. It took me an hour and
a half to convince her. It's not that she doesn't like you.
But she's old. She's set in her ways. And she's worried
about people being around Bella.

ARTY   Me too.

EDDIE   She hasn't even said positively yet. She's thinking
about it. She'll come out. She'll talk to you. She'll see
how it goes. It's up to us to convince her that you two
won't be any trouble . . . That's why I want you both
looking so neat. Don't you see how important this is?

JAY   And what if she *did* take us in? Then you'd be
obligated, Pop. Don't you think you have enough obligations now?

EDDIE   I'm not asking for myself. I'm asking for my boys.
For my boys, I'll be obligated . . . There's nothing to
discuss anymore . . . It's up to Grandma now . . . And
it's up to you. *(He crosses to* GRANDMA's *bedroom door)*
I'll see if she's ready. *(He turns back to them)* If she says
no, I can't take this job. I can't pay back the man I gave
my promise to . . . You're good kids, both of you. Just
show Grandma what a terrific present she's getting to
have you boys live with her . . . Fix your tie, Jay.

Straighten your collar, Arty . . . Stand straight, both of you . . . *(They stand straight. He nods)* That's my boys.

(He goes into GRANDMA'*s room. The boys look at each other)*

JAY   Oh, my God. What if Grandma says "Yes"?

ARTY   She won't. Because I'm going to break something. What's her favorite thing in this room?

JAY   You're not breaking anything. Because we have to stay here and save Pop's life.

ARTY   And what about *our* lives? We could grow up like Aunt Bella. I could be in the seventh grade for the next twenty years.

JAY   Listen, if you act like this when Grandma comes out, that's like putting a gun to Pop's head and pulling the trigger.

ARTY   Oh. So we stay here and get whacked in the head every time we cry . . . or suck candles back on like Aunt Gert. *(He sucks his breath in and says)* "Hello, Arty. How are you?"

JAY *(He grabs* ARTY *by his shirt collar)*   One more word from you and I'll whack you, I swear to God.

    *(*ARTY *pulls away but* JAY *holds on . . . and* ARTY*'s collar gets torn halfway off and dangles there)* Oh, my God. It tore!

ARTY   Well, that's it. The war is over for us . . . I hope
Pop bought the grave next to Mom.

JAY *(Looking in a drawer)*   Jesus! It's all your goddamn
fault . . . Look for a pin, maybe we could stick it back
together.

ARTY   Right. I'm going to be looking in drawers when
Grandma walks in. I'm sure she wants to adopt a couple of crooks.

(*He rushes to* JAY, *but the drawer slams shut and* JAY
howls in pain)

JAY *(Starting to cry)*   Dammit! I hate you so much. I hate
Mom for dying. I hate Pop for putting us in this spot.
I hate Grandma for being such a rotten old lady. I hate
everybody in the whole goddamn world.

(*And the bedroom door opens and* EDDIE *comes out
with a smile*)

EDDIE   You ready, boys? (*And then he looks at them*)
. . . What the hell is going on here? . . . What are you
crying about? What happened to your collar?

(*He quickly closes the bedroom door*)

ARTY   Nothing.

EDDIE   Don't tell me nothing. Were you fighting? Of
course you were fighting, just look at you. I can't believe it. If I can't trust you for two minutes, how can
I trust you for a year? . . . And do you think I would

do this to my mother? To my sister, Bella? . . . I knew this was a stupid idea in the first place. I never would have tried it if I wasn't so desperate . . . I'm ashamed of you. I'm ashamed of you both . . . Wait outside for me. Out in the street. I don't want to look at you . . . Go on, get out.

ARTY   We weren't fighting. It was an accident. I was trying to straighten my tie and I straightened it too tight.

JAY   I was crying about Mom. She'd be so sad to see you in such trouble . . . We really want to stay here. We like Yonkers. We were just praying that Grandma would *let* us stay.

ARTY   Gee, I hope she does . . . It looks like such a nice place to live.

EDDIE   Are you serious? Or are you just trying to lie your way out of this?

JAY   Serious. Very serious.

ARTY   It's the most serious we've been in our lives.

EDDIE   I hope so. For all our sakes . . . Alright. Fix yourself up. Tuck in your collar. Wipe your eyes . . . I'll get Grandma. (*The door opens and* BELLA *comes out. She rushes to the sofa and throws herself on it, sobbing*) Oh, Jesus! Bella? . . . What's wrong? . . . What is it, Bella? (*She buries her face in a pillow like a five-year-old child.* ARTY *and* JAY *look at each other . . .* EDDIE *sits next to* BELLA *and puts his arm around her shoulder. To* BELLA, *softly)* . . . Did Momma say something? . . . Was she angry with you? *(*BELLA *whispers in* EDDIE*'s ear)* No, no, Bella. She does too love your back rubs, she told me that . . . She's just got a lot on her mind today. *(He looks at the boys disapprovingly, then back to* BELLA*)* You alright now, sweetheart? *(*BELLA *whispers again to him)* Yes, I know you're lonely . . . I know it's hard to be alone with her all the time . . . But, Bella, I have good news for you . . . Maybe you won't be alone anymore . . . You know who's going to stay here, Bella? If Momma says yes . . . Arthur and Jay . . . Wouldn't that be nice? . . . To have Arthur and Jay here? . . . They'd live here and spend time with you and you'd have someone to talk to at nights. *(*ARTY *and* JAY *look at each other)* Would you like that, honey?

BELLA *(Beams)* Yes.

EDDIE *(To* BELLA*)* Alright. Then give me a smile and a hug.

*(*BELLA *throws her arms around* EDDIE*'s neck)*

BELLA Don't go away, Eddie . . . Stay and live with us . . . I miss you so much . . . She's so mean sometimes.

EDDIE No, she's not. She's just getting old . . . I can't stay, honey. I have to go away for a while. But the boys will be with you. They're looking forward to it . . . Look how happy they look. *(*ARTY *and* JAY *force two big smiles at her)* . . . Would you like to lie down in your room for a while, Bella? Momma has to talk to the boys now.

BELLA *(Grabs his hand)* No. I want to stay here with you.

EDDIE It would be easier, I think, if Momma and the boys talked alone.

BELLA *(Sternly)* I want to stay here with you.

EDDIE Ohh, God . . . Alright. You sit right there. But you be very quiet now, alright? . . . Just don't interrupt because we don't want to get Momma upset . . . Okay. Here we go.

> *(He crosses to the bedroom door, knocks, and goes in.*
>
> JAY *and* ARTY *look at* BELLA. *She looks up at the ceiling)*

JAY Er . . . Arty and I are really hoping it works out, Aunt Bella.

BELLA *(She puts her finger to her lips)* Shhh. Mustn't interrupt.

JAY Oh, yeah. Right.

> *(*EDDIE *comes out of the bedroom and arranges the boys to greet* GRANDMA*)*

EDDIE Her back is killing her but she doesn't want me to help her. *(He calls in)* Okay, Momma.

> *(There is a beat, as Momma is going to make her entrance when she wants.*

GRANDMA KURNITZ *enters slowly from the bedroom. She is a big woman, or, hopefully, gives that appearance. Not fat, but buxom, with a strong, erect body, despite her seventy-odd years. She has white hair pulled back in European style with buns. She carries a cane and walks with a slight dragging of one foot. She wears rimless glasses and has a pasty-white complexion. She wears a large-print dress of the period with a cameo brooch pinned on. Authority and discipline seem to be her overriding characteristics and she would command attention in a crowd. She speaks with few but carefully chosen words, with a clear German accent.*

She walks to the armchair, not looking at anybody, least of all the boys. Then she sits and looks at EDDIE)

GRANDMA So?

(EDDIE *motions with his head to the boys*)

JAY *(On cue)* Hello, Grandma.

ARTY Hello, Grandma.

(EDDIE *looks at them again and gives them another head signal.* JAY *steps up and kisses her quickly on her cheek and steps back.* ARTY *does the same and steps back.* GRANDMA KURNITZ *hardly reacts*)

EDDIE I know you haven't seen the boys in a long time, Mom. They wanted to come, but with their mother sick so long, they felt they should spend as much time as they could with her . . . I bet they've grown since you've seen them, haven't they?

GRANDMA *(She looks at them, then points her cane at* ARTY*)* Dis iss the little one?

EDDIE Yes. Arthur. He's two years younger, right, Arty?

ARTY Yes. I'm two years younger . . . than him.

GRANDMA *(She looks at* JAY, *points her cane at him)* Dis one I remember more . . . Dis one looks like his mother.

JAY Yes. A lot of people tell me that.

GRANDMA Vot's wrong with your eyes?

JAY My eyes? Oh. They're a little red. I got something in them and I scratched them too hard.

GRANDMA You vere crying maybe?

JAY Me? No. I never cry.

GRANDMA Big boys shouldn't cry.

JAY I know. I haven't cried in years. A couple of times when I was a baby.

EDDIE Oh, they're strong kids, Ma. Both of them.

GRANDMA *(Looks at* JAY*)* Yakob, heh?

JAY Yes, but they call me Jay.

GRANDMA No. I don't like Jay . . . Yakob iss a name.

JAY   Sure. Yakob is fine.

GRANDMA   And Arthur.

ARTY   Arthur. But they call me Arty.

GRANDMA   I don't call you Arty.

ARTY   Sure. I *love* Arthur. Like King Arthur.

GRANDMA   You go to school?

ARTY   Yeah.

GRANDMA   Vat?

ARTY   Yes. I go to the same school as Yakob.

GRANDMA   Vitch one iss da smart one?

(JAY *and* ARTY *look at each other*)

EDDIE   They both do very well in school.

GRANDMA *(She points her cane at* EDDIE*)*   They'll tell me.
(She looks at them) Vitch one iss da smart one?

ARTY *(Pointing to* JAY*)*   Yakob is. He gets A's in everything. I'm better at sports.

GRANDMA   Shports?

ARTY   Baseball. Basketball. Football.

GRANDMA   You play in the mud? In the dirt? You come home with filthy shoes and make marks all over the floor?

ARTY   No. Never. I clean them off at the field. I bring a brush and polish and shine them up on a bench.

(He looks at EDDIE *to see if he got away with that)*

GRANDMA   If the smart one iss smart, he'll make sure you do.

EDDIE   No, the boys are very neat. Even their mother said so.

*(*GRANDMA *taps her cane a few times on the floor, like an announcement)*

GRANDMA   So tell me . . . vy do you vant to live with Grandma?

(The boys look at each other)

ARTY   . . . Why don't *you* tell Grandma, Yakob?

*(*JAY *glares at him)*

JAY   . . . Well . . . because . . . Pop has to go away. And we had to give up our apartment . . . and when Pop said we had the opportunity to live here with you—our only living grandmother . . . and our only living Aunt Bella . . . I thought that families should sort of stick together now that our country is at war with Germ—Japan . . . so we can all be together during times like this . . . and I also think that—no. That's all.

GRANDMA *(Nods)*   Hmm . . . And this is the smart one?

EDDIE   I thought he said that very well, Momma.

GRANDMA *(She points her cane at* ARTY*)*   And what about this King Artur? . . . Vy do you vant to live with Grandma?

ARTY *(After looking at* GRANDMA*)*   . . . Because we have no place else to go.

EDDIE   *Arty!!* . . . I think what Arty is trying to say, Momma—

GRANDMA *(Pointing her cane at* EDDIE*)*   No! . . . he knows vot he vants to say . . . *(She looks at* ARTY*)* I tink maybe *diss* is da smart one.

EDDIE   He's always been very honest. But he's just a boy, Momma—

GRANDMA   So! You haff no place else to go. Dot's vy you vant to live vith Grandma . . . Alright . . . Alright . . . So now Grandma vill tell you vy she doesn't tink you should live vit her . . . Dis house is no place for boys. I'm an old woman. I don't like to talk. I don't like noise. I don't like people in my house. I had six children once, I don't need more again . . . Bella and I take care of the store six days a veek and on Sunday ve rest. Today is Sunday and I'm not resting . . . Bella is not— she's not goot vit people too long. A little bit yes, then she gets too excited . . . You understand vot I'm saying? . . . Vot vould you do here? There's no games in dis house. There's no toys in dis house. I don't like the

35

radio after six o'clock. The news yes, dot's all . . . Ve
go to sleep nine o'clock, ve get up five o'clock. I don't
have friends. Bella don't have friends. You vould not be
happy here. And unhappy boys I don't need.

EDDIE   Momma, can I just say something—?

GRANDMA *(She holds up her cane)*   I'll just say something
. . . I think about dis inside. Because anger hass been
in me for a long time . . . Vy should I do dis? . . . Vot
do I owe your father? . . . Ven did he ever come around
here after he married your mother? I never saw him
. . . Because she turned him against me. His own
mother . . . She didn't like me, I didn't like her. I'm not
afraid to tell da truth either . . . I don't vish anybody's
death. Maybe she vas a goot mother to you, may she
rest in peace, to me she vas nothing . . . And your father
was afraid of her. Dot's vy he stopped coming here.
You're big boys now, how many times haff I seen you
since you were born? Four, five times? . . . Dose are not
grandchildren. Dose are strangers . . . And now he
comes to me for help? . . . He cried in my bedroom. Not
like a man, like a child he cried. He vas always dot vay
. . . I buried a husband and two children und I didn't
cry. I didn't haff time. Bella vas born vit scarlet fever
and she didn't talk until she vas five years old, und I
didn't cry . . . Your father's sister, Gertrude, can't talk
vitout choking und I didn't cry . . . Und maybe one
day, they'll find Louie dead in da street und I von't cry
. . . Dot's how I vas raised. To be strong. Ven dey beat
us vit sticks in Germany ven ve vere children, I didn't
cry . . . You don't survive in dis vorld vitout being like
steel. Your father vants you to grow up, first let *him*
grow up . . . Ven he learns to be a father, like I learned

to be a mother, den he'll be a man. Den he von't need my help . . . You think I'm cruel? You tink I'm a terrible person? Dot a grandmother should say tings like dis? I can see it in your faces vot you tink . . . Goot, it'll make you hard. It'll make you strong. Den you'll be able to take care of yourselves vitout *any*body's help . . . So dot's my decision. Maybe one day you'll tank me for it. *(She gets up)* Give da boys an ice cream cone, Bella. Den come inside and finish my legs.

(She starts for the bedroom. They all stand, stunned.
BELLA, *who has remained seated, seems impervious to this)*

EDDIE *(Without anger)* . . . You're right, Momma. I am the weak one. I am the crybaby . . . Always was. When you wouldn't pick me up and hug me as a child, I cried . . . When my brother and sister died, I cried . . . And I still haven't stopped crying since Evelyn died . . . But you're wrong about one thing. She never turned me against you. She turned me towards *her* . . . To loving, to caring, to holding someone when they needed holding . . . I'm sorry about not bringing the boys out here more. Maybe the reason I didn't was because I was afraid they'd learn something here that I tried to forget . . . Maybe they just learned it today . . . I'm sorry I bothered you on your Sunday. I'm sorry I imposed on your rest. I'm sorry about what they did to you as a child in Berlin. I'm sure it was terrible. But this is Yonkers, Momma. I'm not angry at you for turning me and the boys down. I'm angry at myself for not knowing better . . . Take care of yourself, Momma . . . Never mind the ice cream cones, Bella. I used up all my obligations for this year. *(He crosses to the door)* Come on, boys. We're going. *(JAY and ARTY are too dumbstruck to move, to have been in the middle of all this)* . . . I said let's go.

(They start for the door)

BELLA   Arty? *(She gets up with a warm, sweet smile on her face)* We'll have dinner another night . . . Why don't you and Jay go home and pack your things and I'll get your bed ready and make room in the closet for when you move in.

(The boys stop, look at EDDIE)

EDDIE   Thank you, Bella . . . but Momma and I just decided it's not a good idea.

BELLA   *(Still smiling, she begins to make up the sofa bed)* And, Jay, you make a list of all the things you boys like for breakfast, and I'll make sure we have it . . . And don't forget your toothbrushes because we don't carry them in the store . . . And each of you bring something from your house that you really love, even if it's big, and we'll find someplace to put it.

GRANDMA   Dot's enough, Bella. Diss is not your business.

BELLA   *(To the boys)* How about a picture of your mother? And we can put it right here on the table. It'll be the last thing you see at night and the first thing you see in the morning . . . It's going to be such fun with you both here . . . Momma's right. I do get so excited around people but it makes me so happy.

GRANDMA Bella! Nicht sprecken! Enough!! . . . They're going. Dot's the end of it.

BELLA *(Quite calmly)* No, Momma. They're not going. They're staying. Because if you make them go, I'll go too . . . I know I've said that a thousand times but this time I mean it . . . I could go to the Home. The Home would take me . . . You're always telling me that . . . And if I go, you'll be all alone . . . And you're afraid to be alone, Momma . . . Nobody else knows that but me . . . But you don't have to be, Momma. Because we'll all be together now . . . You and me and Jay and Arty . . . Won't that be fun, Momma?

> *(They stand there, all frozen, except* BELLA, *who is beaming . . .*

> *The stage goes to black)*

Over the sound of the train, in the black, we hear EDDIE'*s voice.*

EDDIE *(Voice-over)*   "Dear Jay and Arty . . . I tried phoning you the other night, but I forgot the phone is in the candy store and you probably couldn't hear it . . . Well, I've been through Kentucky, Georgia, Tennessee, and West Virginia . . . Don't complain about Aunt Bella's cooking to me because I haven't eaten anything down here that wasn't fried, smoked, hashed, gritted, or poned . . . or wasn't caught in a swamp, a tree, or coming out of a hole in the ground . . . Right now I'd go into debt again just to eat an onion roll . . ."

(The lights come up and the letter continues to be read by JAY. *They are both in bed, one lamp on. It is late at night)*

JAY *(He reads)*   "Although business is good, I've had one minor setback. I've developed what the doctor calls an irregular heartbeat. He says it's not serious, but doesn't think I should be traveling so much. But I can't afford to stop now." *(He looks at* ARTY*)* An irregular heartbeat doesn't sound too good . . . God, I wish there was some way we could make some money. Not "kid" money. I mean *real* money.

ARTY   What if one night we cut off Grandma's braids and sold it to the army for barbed wire?

JAY   I can't believe we're fighting a war to make this a better world for someone like you.

(The front door opens and BELLA *comes in, closing the door quietly. She looks at the boys and puts her finger to her lips to be quiet)*

BELLA   Is Grandma sleeping? Don't tell me, you'll wake her up . . . Arty! Jay! The most wonderful and exciting thing happened to me tonight. But don't ask me. I can't tell you. You're my good luck charms, both of you.

GRANDMA   *(Appearing suddenly out of her room. To* BELLA*)* You tink I don't hear you coming up the stairs? You tink I don't know it's eleven o'clock? You tink I don't know where you've been?

BELLA   Just to the movies, Ma.

GRANDMA   Movies, movies, movies. You waste your money and your life in da movies. Und den you walk home by yourself. Do you know what kind of men are on the street at eleven o'clock?

BELLA   I didn't see a soul, Ma.

GRANDMA   Ya, ya, ya! Look for trouble, you'll find trouble.

BELLA   No one bothers me, Ma.

GRANDMA   Then you waste money on movie magazines? Fill your head with Hollywood and dreams that don't happen to people like us?

BELLA   Sometimes they do.

GRANDMA   Never. NEVER!! . . . *(Holding out her hand)* Give it to me. I don't want trash in this house.

BELLA   It's my magazine, Ma. I bought it with my own money.

GRANDMA   No! *My* money. I pay for everything here. You don't have anything unless I give you. Give— me—the—magazine!

BELLA   Please don't do this to me in front of the boys, Momma.

GRANDMA   You bring it home in front of the boys, you'll give me the magazine in front of the boys. *(Holds her hand out)* Give it to me now, Bella. (BELLA *looks at the boys, embarrassed, then gives her the magazine.* GRANDMA *looks at the magazine and nods in disgust)* When I'm dead, you can buy your own magazine.

BELLA   No, I won't, Momma. Because you'll find a way to get them anyway.

(She rushes into her room. GRANDMA *looks at the boys)*

GRANDMA   . . . You like to pay my electric bill? (JAY *quickly turns out the light. It is dark, except for the light from* GRANDMA's *room)* . . . And you try cutting my braids off, you'll get your fingers chopped off.

(She goes in and slams her door.

The lights go to black and we hear the train again)

SCENE 3

In the dark, we hear the voice of EDDIE *again.*

EDDIE *(Voice-over)* "Dear Boys . . . This'll just have to be a short one. I'm in Houston, Texas, and I just got plumb tuckered out. That's how they talk down here. I had to take a week off and rest. Nothing to worry about. I'll be on the road again real soon and I promise I'll make up the time . . . Love, Pop."

> *(The lights come up. It is Sunday afternoon, weeks later.* ARTY *stands on* GRANDMA's *chair, his hand upraised, and he is jubilant)*

ARTY *(Yelling)* Alone at last!! Grandma's out! Aunt Bella's out! We have the house to ourselves. We're *free!* Ya ya ya ya ya!!!

JAY Will you shut up! She could walk back in any minute. You know what she'd do if she found you jumping on her chair?

ARTY *(With German accent)* Ya! She vould chop off my legs . . . And Aunt Bella vould cook dem for dinner.

> *(He jumps on the bed)*

JAY *(Looks out the window)* Hey! Arty! There's that car again.

ARTY What car?

JAY The black Studebaker. It's the two guys who came looking for Uncle Louie. They look like killers to me . . . What do you think they want?

ARTY (*Looks out the window*) I don't know. Let's give 'em Grandma. Ya ya ya ya ya!

JAY (*Pulling him away*) Get out of there. (*He peeks again*) They just keep circling and circling. Aren't you afraid of guys like that?

ARTY No. I lived up here for a month. I can take anything.

(*The front door opens and* BELLA *comes in*)

BELLA Is Momma home?

JAY No. She's still at Aunt Gert's.

BELLA I don't want to cry. I don't want to cry. I don't want to cry.

JAY Is there anything we can do? . . . You can talk to us, Aunt Bella.

BELLA Do you think so? Do you think I can trust you? You're still so young.

JAY You don't have to be old to be trusting.

BELLA And you'd never tell Grandma what I tell you? Because if she ever found out, she'd put me in the Home . . . She would. For the rest of my life.

JAY I don't think she would do that. She just says that to scare you sometimes.

BELLA   No. She would do it. Sometimes she'd take me on the trolley, and we'd go by the Home and she'd say, "That's where you'll live if you're not a good girl."

ARTY   You said she wouldn't do that because she's afraid to be alone.

BELLA   But she's not alone anymore. She's got you two here.

ARTY   Oh, no. If you left, we'd go with you to the Home.

JAY   Arty, knock it off . . . If you don't want to tell us, Aunt Bella, you don't have to. We're your friends.

BELLA   No. I have to tell somebody . . . I wish Eddie was here. Eddie would know what to do.

JAY   We're Eddie's sons. That's almost the same thing.

BELLA   Yes. That's true . . . Alright . . . Come here. Sit down, both of you. *(She crosses to the sofa bed and sits. They sit on either side of her)* This is our secret now, alright? . . . A sacred secret. Say it, the both of you.

ARTY and JAY and BELLA   This is a sacred secret.

BELLA   Alright then . . . *(She smiles)* I'm going to get married . . . I'm going to be a wife and I'm going to have lots and lots of children and live in a place of my own . . . Isn't that wonderful news? *(The boys look at each other)* You're the only ones that know this . . . Jay! Arty! I'm going to get married.

   (They are, of course, dumbstruck)

JAY   Gee, that's swell, Aunt Bella.

ARTY   Have you met anybody yet?

BELLA   What do you mean, have I met anyone? . . . Of
course I have . . . I met him ten days ago at the movies.
At the Orpheum Theatre . . . I saw him there four times
this week.

JAY   You both went to the same movie four times?

BELLA   I didn't mind. And he has to, because he works
there. He's an usher . . . And he looks so wonderful in
his uniform.

ARTY   He's an usher?

BELLA   And his name is Johnny. I always thought I
would marry someone named Johnny.

ARTY   What a great guess.

BELLA   Anyway, we went out later for some coffee
. . . And we went for walks in the park . . . and down
near the river. And then today, just like in the movies,
at exactly two o'clock . . . or two-fifteen . . . or two-
thirty . . . he asked me to marry him . . . And I said I
would have to think it over, but the answer was yes.

ARTY   That was pretty quick thinking it over.

BELLA   I know. I didn't want him to change his mind
. . . Are you as happy about this as I am?

JAY   Oh, sure . . . sure . . . sure . . . How old is he?

BELLA   He's thirty . . . Maybe not. Maybe about forty
. . . But he's so handsome. And so polite. And quiet. I
had to do all of the talking. All he said was, "Would
you marry me?"

JAY   Was he ever married before?

BELLA   Oh, no. I would never marry someone who was
married before. I want it to be the first time for both
of us.

JAY   If he has no children, how come he's not in the
army?

BELLA   Oh, he wanted to go but they wouldn't take him
because of his handicap.

JAY   What handicap?

BELLA   He has a reading handicap.

JAY   You mean he has bad eyes?

BELLA   No. He just has trouble learning things. The way
I did. He went to a special school when he was a boy.
The one near the Home. He was there once, in the
Home, for about six months, and he said it was terrible
. . . So his parents took him out . . . And now he's much
happier.

ARTY   Oh, I get it . . . Do you get it, Jay?

JAY   I can tell why you're not anxious to tell Grandma
. . . I mean, because it's so sudden like.

BELLA   And he doesn't want to be an usher forever . . . He wants to open up a restaurant. Because he said the one thing people always have to do is eat. Don't you agree? (ARTY *and* JAY *nod together*) . . . I would be the cook and he would be the manager. I would love that more than anything in the whole world.

JAY   Could he do that? Manage a restaurant? If he couldn't read the menus?

BELLA   Well, I would do all that. I would help him . . . The only thing is, his parents are poor and he doesn't make much money and we'd need about five thousand dollars to open a restaurant . . . And I don't know if Momma would give it to me.

JAY   Your mother has five thousand dollars?

BELLA   Oh, more. Ten or fifteen thousand. I'm not supposed to tell anyone.

JAY   Where does she keep it? In the bank?

BELLA   No. It's here in the house somewhere. She changes the hiding place every year. No one knows she has it . . . Not Eddie or Gert or Louie. No one . . . So my problem is, I have to get her to say yes to marrying Johnny, and yes to opening the restaurant and moving away, and yes to giving me the five thousand dollars. But I don't think she's going to say yes, do you?

JAY   I don't think she's going to let you go to the movies much anymore.

BELLA   She won't know if you don't tell her. You won't tell her, will you, Jay?

JAY   I swear.

BELLA   Arty?

ARTY   She and I have very short conversations.

BELLA   I have to go inside now and think this out. I'm not good at thinking things out. I'm much better with my hands . . . But you're smart. Both of you. Maybe you'll think it out for me . . . Please do. I'd be grateful to you for the rest of my life. *(She starts to go, then stops)* Oh. I thought of a name for the restaurant, too . . . "La Bella Johnnie."

JAY   That's nice.

BELLA   Yeah. I just hope he can read it. *(She goes into her bedroom)*

ARTY   Wait'll he meets Grandma. He'll be back in the Home in a week.

JAY   Fifteen thousand!! Wow! You think she would have loaned some of it to Pop. *(Looking around)* Where would be the safest place to hide it? Where no one would think of looking?

ARTY   You're not really thinking of stealing it, are you?

JAY   No, but what if we just borrowed it? I would just love to send Pop an envelope with nine thousand dollars in it.

ARTY   And who would he think sent it to him? *God???*

JAY   He had an uncle in Poland who died. He left the money in his will for Pop.

ARTY   You think the Germans would let some Jew in Poland send nine thousand dollars to some Jew in Alabama?

Blackout

We hear the train . . . then EDDIE's *voice . . .*

EDDIE *(Voice-over)* ". . . Dear Boys . . . Traveling through the South has been a whole new education for me. Some people are very warm and polite and educated and very well spoken. And then there are some on the train who spit tobacco juice on the windows . . . A lot of people have trouble with my New York accent. I didn't even know I had one till I got here . . . I met a nice Jewish family in Atlanta, but I couldn't understand them either. This woman, Mrs. Schneider, said to me, 'You all come over to the synagogue this Shabuss and you'll meet some mighty fine folks.' I didn't want to hurt her feelings so I said, 'Sho nuff.' And she just looked at me and said, 'Who's Shonuff?' . . . I guess it takes a while to learn the dialect. Love, Pop."

> *(The lights come up. It is one week later, about twelve o'clock at night. The room is dark except for the full moon that shines brightly in through the window.*
>
> *The boys' bed is open; Neither of them is in it.* ARTY, *in pajamas, is standing near the door that leads downstairs)*

ARTY Jay! Hurry up! What if Grandma wakes up? . . . This is crazy. Why would she hide money in the store?

> *(Suddenly, we see the flashlight coming from downstairs.* ARTY *rushes back into bed.* JAY *comes in with the flashlight)*

51

JAY I looked everywhere. There's no money down there. *(He shivers)* God, I'm freezing. I was looking under the ice cream cartons. *(He gets into bed)* I think I got frostbite.

ARTY Why would she keep money under ice cream? We use those cartons up every week.

JAY Not the boysenberry. Boysenberry sits there for months. Nobody's ever going to look under boysenberry.

ARTY I can't believe we're stealing money from our own grandmother.

> *(They put out the flashlight and turn to go to sleep ... A moment passes ... Then the front door opens. We see a man in a hat enter, closing the door, then slowly, quietly cross toward the window. He carries a small black bag)*

JAY Who's that?

> *(Turning the flashlight on the man)*

LOUIE Get that light outa my face and go back to sleep, kid.

JAY There's nothing here to steal, mister. I swear.

LOUIE Is that you, Jay?

JAY Yeah. Who are you?

LOUIE It's Uncle Louie.

JAY   Uncle Louie? No kidding? . . . Arty! It's Uncle
Louie.

ARTY   Uncle Louie? . . . Really? Hi, Uncle Louie.

LOUIE   Is that Arty?

ARTY   Yeah. It's Arty . . . Hi, Uncle Louie.

LOUIE   Wait a second. (LOUIE *turns on the lamp.* LOUIE
KURNITZ *is about thirty-six years old. He wears a double-
breasted suit with a hanky in the breast pocket, black
pointy shoes, a dark blue shirt, and a loud tie. He also wears
a fedora hat and carries a small black satchel, not unlike
a doctor's bag)* Whaddya know? Look at you! Couple
a big guys now, ain't you? . . . You don't come around
for a while and you grow up on me . . . Come here.
Come on. I want a hug. You heard me. Move it. *(The
boys look at each other, not thinking LOUIE was the hug-
ging type. They quickly climb out of bed and go to him.
He puts his arms around both their shoulders and pulls
them in to him. He looks at JAY)* Picture of your mother.
Pretty woman, your mother . . . *(To ARTY)* And you.
You look like a little bull terrier. Is that what you are,
a bull terrier? *(He musses ARTY's hair)*

ARTY   Yeah, I guess so.

LOUIE   *(Fakes a punch at JAY's midsection)* Hey, watch it!
What are you now, a middleweight or what? Who's
been beefin' you up?

JAY   Aunt Bella. She's a good cook.

LOUIE *(Taking off his hat)*   And a couple a midnight trips down to the ice cream freezer, heh? Diggin' into the boysenberry with your flashlight? . . . That's breakin' and enterin', kid. Two to five years.

JAY   You saw me?

LOUIE *(Crosses to* GRANDMA's *door and listens)*   I been down there since Ma closed the store.

JAY   Sitting in the dark?

LOUIE   Yeah. Waitin' for her to go to sleep. I wasn't in no mood for long conversations.

JAY *(Looks at* ARTY, *then at* LOUIE*)*   I just took a fingerful, that's all. I love boysenberry.

LOUIE   Big mistake, kid. Mom reads fingerprints. She'll nail you in the morning.

JAY   Are you serious?

LOUIE   Get outa here. What are you? A couple a push-overs? Like your old man . . . What'd he bring up for you, Arty? A thumbful of pistachio?

ARTY   No. Nothing. I wasn't hungry.

LOUIE   You think your pop and I didn't do that when we were kids? That was the beauty part. Never took nothin' durin' the day. A ton a ice cream, a store full a candy, anything we wanted. Never took nothin' . . . But as soon as Ma let her braids down and turned out the lights, we were down there lappin' up the cream and meowin' like cats . . . Ain't that the way? It's only fun when there's a chance a gettin' caught. Nothin' sweeter than danger, boys, am I right?

JAY I guess so.

LOUIE Damn right.

ARTY I didn't know Pop was like that.

LOUIE Yeah, well, he was no good at it anyway. Ma knew what was goin' on. She could tell if there was salt missin' from a pretzel . . . But she wouldn't say nothin'. She'd come up from the store with the milk, siddown for breakfast, knowin' that two scoops of everything was missin', and she'd just stare at you . . . right into your eyeballs, pupil to pupil . . . never blinkin' . . . Her eyes looked like two district attorneys . . . and Eddie couldn't take the pressure. He'd always crack. Tears would start rollin' down his cheeks like a wet confession . . . and Whack, he'd get that big German hand right across the head . . . But not me. I'd stare her right back until her eyelids started to weigh ten pounds each . . . And she'd turn away from me, down for the count . . . And you know what? She loved it . . . because I knew how to take care of myself . . . Yeah, me and Ma loved to put on the gloves and go the distance.

(He takes off his jacket and puts it on the back of the chair)

JAY Nobody told us you were coming over tonight.

LOUIE Nobody knew. It was even a surprise for me. I gotta stay here a couple days, maybe a week. They're paintin' my apartment.

ARTY You didn't know they were going to paint your apartment?

LOUIE They just found the right color paint tonight. Hard to find with the war on. *(He takes off his jacket, revealing a holster with a pistol in it)* So, you kids been keepin' your nose outa trouble?

(The boys look at the gun, mesmerized)

JAY Huh?

LOUIE How's Pop? Ma tells me he's in the junk business. Is that right, Arty?

ARTY *(Looking at the gun)* Huh?

LOUIE Sellin' scrap iron or somethin', ain't that it?

BOTH BOYS Huh?

LOUIE Whatsamatter? *(He looks at the gun)* This? *(He smiles)* Hey, don't worry about it. *(He takes it out of its holster)* I'm holdin' it for a friend. This policeman I know went on vacation, he didn't want to lose it. They have to pay for it when they lose it . . . *(He puts it in his pants, under the belt, just over the fly)* Also, the ladies like it. You dance with 'em close, gives 'em a thrill.

(He winks at them)

JAY Is it . . . is it loaded?

LOUIE Gee, I hope not. If it went off, I'd have to become a ballerina. *(He winks at the boys. He hangs the gun and holster on a chair, comes back, and resumes getting undressed)* Does your pop ever send you some loose change once in a while?

JAY Oh, yeah. Whenever he can.

LOUIE Like never, right? You think I don't know what's goin' on? The sharks are puttin' the bite on him, right? He shoulda come to me. There's lotsa ways of borrowin' money. Your pop don't unnerstand that. Sometimes bein' on the up and up just gets you down and down, know what I mean, Jay?

JAY Yeah . . . I never knew a policeman could lend his gun to someone.

LOUIE *(Looks at him, then at* ARTY*)* You got a smart brother there, Arty, you know that? You're right, Jay. It's my gun. I'm a bodyguard for a very prominent and distinguished political figure. It's sort of like an FBI man, only they call it something else.

ARTY You mean a henchman?

LOUIE *(Glaring at him)* Who's been telling you stories like that? Jay?

ARTY No. I swear.

LOUIE Don't ever repeat that word around to anyone again, you understand?

ARTY   I didn't mean to say it. I was thinking of hunch-back.

LOUIE   A couple of jokers here, heh? Don't pull my leg, Arty, it might come off in your hands . . . So, we got a little business to discuss. You boys got any problem with makin' a little after-school money?

JAY   You mean a job? I've been looking, but Grandma wants us in the store after school. To help pay our expenses.

LOUIE   Tell you what. How'd you like to work for me? Five bucks a week, split between you, cash on the barrel. Only first you gotta guess what number I'm thinkin' of. Make a mistake and the deal's off . . . Take a guess, boys.

ARTY   Three.

JAY   Seven.

LOUIE   Thirty-seven. That's right. Good guess. You're on Louie's payroll now. *(He takes a five-dollar bill out of his garter and hands it to JAY)* . . . Now, Arty, can you drive a car?

ARTY   Me? I'm only thirteen and a half.

LOUIE   Too bad. I need someone who can drive a car.

ARTY   I'm a pretty good roller skater.

LOUIE *(He smiles)*   That's good, 'cause I'm spinnin' your wheels, kid. Now your leg's bein' pulled. Wake up and live. It's a fast world out there.

JAY Uncle Louie . . . This five-dollar bill . . . It has your picture on it.

LOUIE *(To* ARTY*)* He ain't no faster than you. Look in your pocket, Arty.

(ARTY *feels in his pajama pocket and takes out a five-dollar bill, unfolded)*

ARTY It's five dollars. A real one. How'd you do that?

LOUIE These fingers were touched by genius. I could have been a concert violinist, but the handkerchief kept fallin' off my neck.

JAY What do we have to do for the money?

LOUIE Nothin'. Like if anyone comes around here lookin' for me, you don't know nothin', you ain't seen nothin', you ain't heard nothin'. You think you can handle that?

ARTY There were two men here the other day looking for you.

LOUIE Yeah? What'd they look like?

ARTY One had a broken nose and the other one had—

LOUIE —a Betty Grable tie.

ARTY Right.

LOUIE Hollywood Harry. Got all the stars hand-painted on silk. He's got a Gypsy Rose Lee tie you can see when you get a little older . . . So if they show up here again askin' questions, what do you say to 'em?

BOTH   Nothing.

LOUIE   Smart boys. Look in Jay's pocket, Arty.

(ARTY *looks in* JAY*'s pocket, takes out a bill*)

ARTY   Another five dollars.

LOUIE   I could have played Carnegie Hall.

JAY   We wouldn't be doing anything wrong, would we?

LOUIE   You're my brother's kids, you think I'm gonna get you involved with somethin' stupid? Don't be stupid. There's a couple of guys who don't like me 'cause I've been seein' a lady I shouldn't a been seeing. A minor neighborhood problem . . . Okay. It's late. I'm gonna wash up. We'll bunk up together tonight, okay?

ARTY   Sure. There's plenty of room.

LOUIE   Oh. One last thing. *(Pointing to his black satchel)* Don't touch this. I got my valuables in there. My draft card. My driver's license . . . My good cuff links. I'll put it somewhere you won't have to worry about it. *(He starts for the bathroom with the bag, then stops)* Oh, Arty. See if there's anything else in your pajama bottoms.

ARTY *(Looks)*   No. There's nothing there.

LOUIE   Well, don't worry. You're young yet.

(He chuckles and goes into the bathroom)

ARTY   He's incredible. It's like having a James Cagney movie in your own house.

JAY   We're not taking that money. They're not painting his apartment at midnight. He's a bagman and he's got a bag and a gun and Pop wouldn't want us to get paid for saying "Nothin' " to Hollywood Harry in the Betty Grable tie. Forget it.

(BELLA's door opens and she comes out quietly)

BELLA   Jay? Arty? Have you thought of anything yet? About how I should tell Grandma about you-know-who?

JAY   Gee. No. We've been very busy ourselves.

BELLA   Sure. I understand. But if you *do* think of something, I'm going to give you each a dollar. I know you could use it. I'll let you go back to sleep. I was having such a good dream. I'm gonna go back and finish it.

(She goes back in her room and closes the door)

JAY   You know, we could make a great living just from this family.

(The bathroom door opens and LOUIE comes out carrying his black bag. He puts it where he can see it from the bed, then sits, takes off his garters and socks, and gets into bed)

LOUIE   You guys have to go to the bathroom?

JAY   No. Why?

LOUIE   I don't like anybody getting up while I'm sleeping.

ARTY   Sure . . . How late do you sleep?

LOUIE   Until I see something I don't like.

JAY   You can see while you're sleeping?

LOUIE *(Smiles)*   Don't try me, kid. I wake up grouchy.
(He looks around contentedly) Yeah, it's good to be
home. In my own bed.

ARTY   Is this where *you* slept?

LOUIE   Yeah. Me and Eddie. And Gert slept with Bella.
And Ma slept with her cane . . . There's nothing like
family, boys. The one place in the world you're safe,
is with your family . . . Right?

JAY   Right.

ARTY   Right.

LOUIE   Right. So unless something unforeseen goes
wrong, I'll see you in the morning, pals . . . *(He turns
out the lamp)* Sleep tight.

> *(He turns on his side, away from them. There is a
> silence . . . then:)*

ARTY   Jay?

JAY What?

ARTY I have to go to the bathroom.

LOUIE *(Without moving)* Save it.

(In the dark we hear:)

EDDIE *(Voice-over)* "Dear Boys . . . The one thing that keeps me going is knowing you're with my family. Thank God you're in good hands. Love, Pop."

Curtain

Act Two

In the dark, we hear the "train" music and a letter from EDDIE.

As the lights come up, we see ARTY *in bed, wrapped up in a bathrobe, a comic book on his lap. He is reading a letter as* EDDIE'*s voice continues:*

EDDIE *(Voice-over)*   "Dear Boys . . . Sorry I haven't kept up my letter writing. The truth is, I was in the hospital a few days. Nothing serious. The doctor said it was just exhaustion. I remember when I was a boy, if I got sick, my mother used to give me the worst tasting German mustard soup. God, how I hated it. Luckily, they don't serve it in Mississippi. I'll write soon. Love, Pop."

>   *(The front door opens and* JAY *comes in carrying a bowl of soup)*

JAY   You got it real rough. Reading comic books and missing school. I wish *I* had a fever. Here. Drink this.

ARTY *(Looking at it suspiciously)*   What is it?

JAY   Grandma made you soup.

ARTY   Forget it. I'm not drinking it.

JAY   Don't start in with her, Arty. She's in a rotten mood today.

ARTY   You mean all those other days she was in a *good* mood?

JAY   Just drink it . . . Where's Uncle Louie?

ARTY   Taking a nap in Aunt Bella's room.

JAY   Well, tell him he got a phone call this morning. One of the guys from the Studebaker.

ARTY   But you said you don't know nothin', right?

JAY   Right. And he said, "You tell Louie that Friday night the dance is over."

ARTY   What dance?

JAY   The "Goodbye Louie" dance.

ARTY   You mean he's double-crossing the mob?

JAY   You got it.

ARTY   Wow! . . . You think they're going to kill him?

JAY   Maybe all three of us. We work for him, don't we?

(*The front door opens.* GRANDMA *walks in wearing her candy store apron, looking angry*)

GRANDMA (*To* JAY)   It takes twenty minutes to bring up soup? . . . I got one sweeper not sweeping downstairs, I don't need two.

JAY   I was just going.

GRANDMA   And don't let the kids sit on the stool all day. One buys a malted and the other two steal pretzels. If they steal, you pay for it.

JAY Sure. That's only fair.

(He crosses to the front door)

GRANDMA Vot was dot?

JAY I said, "Yes, I hear."

GRANDMA He's fresh to me, dat one. *(She pulls the covers off of* ARTY*)* Come on. Out of da bed. It's enough lying around already.

ARTY *(He pulls the sheet back up)* I'm freezing. And I'm burning up with fever. You can feel my head.

GRANDMA You lay in bed, you get fever. You get up und walk, da fever looks for somebody else. *(She hits the bed with her cane twice)* Out! Out!

ARTY *(He gets out of bed, stands, and shivers)* My mother always kept me in bed when I had a fever.

GRANDMA *(She straightens the sheets and starts to fold the bed back into a sofa)* You're not in your mother's house no more. *(Pointing to the chair at the living room table)* You sit in dat chair and you do your homevork. And no funny books. And you finish dat soup. All of it.

ARTY I tried. I can't get it down.

GRANDMA If you eat it qvick, you von't taste it.

ARTY I would taste this if I didn't have a tongue.

GRANDMA   You listen to me. You're not fresh yet like da other one, but I see it coming. No, sir. Not in dis house . . . You live vith me, you don't stay in bed two days . . . You get better qvick und you get dressed und you come downstairs und you vash up the soda fountain und you sveep up the store. I didn't ask to take care of you, but if I take care of you, you'll do vot I tell you. *Don't turn away from me!* You'll look at me!! . . . You're not going to vin dis argument, I tell you dot right now. You understand me?

ARTY   . . . Yes.

GRANDMA   Den put da soup in your mouth right now or I do it for you.

(*He looks at her. She obviously means business. He quickly puts the soup in his mouth. He keeps it there*)

ARTY   . . . I can't swallow it. (GRANDMA *crosses to him, pulls his head back, and the soup goes down*) You could drown me like that . . . Why are you so mean to me? I'm your own grandson.

GRANDMA   Dot's right. And vot am I?

ARTY   What do you mean?

GRANDMA   *Vot am I??* . . . Am I a nobody?

ARTY   No. You're my grandmother.

GRANDMA   Den vere's da respect? Da respect I never got from you or your family since da day you vere born?

ARTY   You're just mad at my mother and you're taking
it out on me. You don't care about your rotten soup or
making me get better. You just want me to be miserable
because somebody made you miserable in Germany.
Even Pop said it . . . Well, that's not my fault. Take it
out on Hitler, not on me.

GRANDMA   Und if you vere a boy growing up in Germany, you vould be dead by now.

ARTY   That's right. Maybe I would. And if I ate this
soup, I would be just as dead. Would that make you
happy then? You want to be happy, Grandma? Watch!
(And he quickly eats six or seven spoonfuls of the soup)
Okay? Now you can stand there and watch me die.

GRANDMA   No. You von't die. You'll be better dis after-
noon. It's not so important dat you hate me, Artur
. . . It's only important dat you live. *(She crosses to the
door and opens it)* Dot's something dot I could never
teach your father.

    (She exits.

    BELLA's *bedroom door opens and* LOUIE *comes out
    with sleepy eyes and mussed hair. He wears an under-
    shirt, pants, and socks, no shoes)*

LOUIE   Ever hear of General Rommel?

ARTY   Who?

LOUIE   General Irwin Rommel. German tank com-
mander. Right now he's rollin' right across Egypt, cut-

tin' through the whole British army. Tough as they come . . . But if Momma wanted him to eat the soup, he would eat the soup.

ARTY Did you eat it when you were a kid?

LOUIE Oh, yeah.

ARTY I thought you weren't afraid of her.

LOUIE I wasn't. That's how I proved it to her. I hated that soup worse than you. But I would drink three bowls of it and ask for more. She knew she couldn't win with me.

ARTY I wish I was as tough as you.

LOUIE Hey, you're gettin' there. You took her on, kid. That took guts. That took moxie.

ARTY What's moxie?

(LOUIE *stands in a defiant position, in his body and in his face)*

LOUIE *That's* moxie! . . . Where's Jay-Jay?

ARTY Downstairs guarding the pretzels . . . Uncle Louie . . . There was a telephone call for you.

LOUIE For me?

ARTY Jay took it. He told them he never heard of you.

LOUIE But they left a message, right?

ARTY   Yeah. They said, "Tell Louie that Friday night the dance is over."

LOUIE *(Smiles)*   Yeah. Well, that don't mean nothin'. A couple a Bronx boys like to talk tough. It's just horsin' around. You know what I mean? Huh? . . . Whatsa matter? Grandma got you down?

ARTY   I think she loves doing it.

LOUIE   Hey, let me tell you somethin'. Guess who hates livin' here more than you? *(He points to* GRANDMA's *door)* The old lady with the cane. That's right. Grandma hates runnin' this store. She hates livin' in Yonkers. You know how many friends she's made here in thirty years? . . . Zippo.

ARTY   She doesn't exactly put herself out with people.

LOUIE   I never said she was a lot a laughs. I'll tell you the truth. I don't like her much myself. She knows it. Why should I? She used to lock me in a closet for breakin' a dish. A ten-cent dish, I'd get two, three hours in the closet. And if I cried, I'd get another hour . . . No light, no water, just enough air to breathe. That's when I learned not to cry. And after a few times in the closet, I toughened up. But I also never broke another dish . . . No, I didn't like her, but I respected her. Hell of a teacher, Ma was.

ARTY   Wouldn't it have been easier if she bought paper plates?

LOUIE   Then where's the lesson? There's no respect for paper plates. Hear me out . . . She was no harder on us

73

than she was on herself. When she was twelve years old, her old man takes her to a political rally in Berlin. The cops broke it up. With sticks, on horseback. Someone throws a rock, a cop bashes in her old man's head, a horse goes down and crushes Ma's foot. Nobody ever fixed it. It hurts every day of her life but I never once seen her take even an aspirin . . . She coulda had an operation but she used the money she saved to get to this country with her husband and six kids. That's moxie, kid.

ARTY   Did she ever put my father in the closet?

LOUIE   Not a chance. She'd open the closet door and he'd tie himself to the radiator. Even if it was hot. No, he was too afraid to go up against her. He was careful. He never broke nothin' except maybe himself . . .

ARTY   Didn't you ever want to run away?

LOUIE   I did. Twelve times. Still a record in Yonkers. The last time she wouldn't take me back. Told the policeman she didn't know me. I had no place to go so I lived under the house with a couple of cats for two weeks. Dead of winter. Bella would come out and bring me sandwiches, a blanket, couple a candles. Mom caught her and put her in the closet overnight. But Bella don't understand anything so she thought it was kinda fun. Or maybe she thought it was the safest place to be . . . Now, Gert—Gert was more scared than your old man. Gert used to talk in her sleep and Mom heard her one night sayin' things she didn't like. So Gert didn't get supper that week. Until she learned to sleep holdin' her breath.

ARTY   I don't blame you for hating her.

LOUIE   I didn't say "hate." I didn't *like* her. That's different. How you feelin'?

ARTY   I think my fever's gone.

LOUIE   Lousy soup but it works . . . When Jay comes up, tell him to bring me some coffee and a doughnut. I'll be in the shower. I wanna clean up before I go.

ARTY   You're leaving? When?

LOUIE   Tonight. No point waitin' till the dance is over.

   (He winks, then starts for the bathroom)

ARTY   Uncle Louie . . . ? *(LOUIE stops)* Are you in trouble?

LOUIE *(He smiles)*   Arty! I was never *not* in trouble.

   (He goes into bathroom and closes the door.

   The front door opens and JAY *storms in, looking furious. He slams the door closed)*

JAY   I hate her! . . . I hate her guts. No wonder Mom never wanted us to come here.

ARTY   What did she do?

JAY   She charged me for three pretzels. Three pretzels that some kids stole while she was downstairs and I was upstairs with your soup . . . She says, "No, there were twelve pretzels in the glass when I went upstairs and nine pretzels when I came down." . . . Not even Sherlock Holmes would notice that . . .

ARTY Two cents a pretzel, it's only six cents.

JAY Oh, is that all it is? Then *you* pay it . . . Is Uncle Louie still sleeping?

ARTY He's taking a shower. He's leaving tonight.

JAY Leaving? I have to talk to him.

ARTY About what?

JAY It's private business.

ARTY Jay, you don't *have* any business. All you got is a job that costs you six cents a day . . . Come on, tell me, Jay. I'll find out sooner or later.

JAY . . . I'm going to ask Uncle Louie to take me with him.

ARTY *WHAT???*

JAY Will you be quiet!

ARTY Are you crazy? Go with Uncle Louie?

JAY I have to make money. Get a good job somewhere. But I can't leave here with minus six cents in my pocket. Uncle Louie is my ticket out.

ARTY Running away. That's all Pop has to hear.

JAY Well, we just can't count on Pop anymore. Maybe I can take care of him better than he's taking care of us.

ARTY Doing what?

JAY Maybe Uncle Louie can teach me a few things.

ARTY Oh, great. To become what? A junior bagman? "The Pocketbook Kid"?

JAY If Uncle Louie says yes, you can't stop me.

ARTY . . . Then take me with you.

JAY Take *you?* You're only a kid. Besides, she doesn't treat you the way she treats me.

ARTY I'm afraid of her, Jay. A horse fell on her when she was a kid and she hasn't taken an aspirin yet.

JAY Look, if I can get set up somewhere with a good-paying job, I'll send for you.

ARTY You promise?

JAY I swear on Momma's grave.

ARTY Artur and Yakob, the gangsters. I can't believe it.

(The front door opens and BELLA *comes in)*

BELLA *(To* JAY*)* Oh, here you are. Momma sent me up to look for you. She didn't know where you were for twenty minutes.

JAY I'm coming right down. I just have to ask Uncle Louie something. He's in the shower.

BELLA *(To* ARTY*)* Are you feeling better, Arty?

ARTY Oh. Much.

BELLA No more fever?

ARTY No. It got scared away.

BELLA I'm glad. Because we're having company tonight. My sister Gertrude. Do you remember her?

JAY Sort of.

BELLA She hasn't been well. She doesn't breathe right. I think it's because she used to sleep with her head inside the pillow.

ARTY *Inside?*

(BELLA *nods, quickly closes the front door, then crosses closer to the boys*)

BELLA *(Whispering)* Tonight's the night.

JAY Tonight's what night?

BELLA The night that I talk to Momma. About you-know-what.

JAY Just the two of you?

BELLA   No. With Aunt Gertrude and Uncle Louie here. And you and Arty. I wouldn't dare talk to Momma without the family here. To back me up . . . You *are* going to back me up, aren't you? You promised.

JAY   It's not going to go very late, is it?

BELLA   Not if everybody backs me up . . . You're not going anyplace, are you?

JAY   Me? No. Where would *I* be going?

BELLA   My heart hasn't stopped pounding all day. I'm so nervous, I can't stop eating. I ate three pretzels before and I *never* eat pretzels.

JAY   *You* ate the pretzels? . . . If you eat anything else, would you tell Grandma first?

BELLA   Oh, she knows I ate the pretzels. She even said to me, "Why are you eating so much? You nervous about something?" . . . I'd better get downstairs. *(She crosses to the door)* You too, Jay. I don't want to do anything to upset Momma before tonight. *(She opens the door)* Arty, if you want more soup, just let me know.

   (She goes and closes the door)

JAY *(Furious)*   She *knew* Aunt Bella ate the pretzels!! . . . Grandma's crazy, Arty. Where did that horse fall, on her *head?*

   (LOUIE comes out of the bathroom, his hair wet and combed straight back. He has a towel around his neck and he carries the little black satchel)

LOUIE   Perfect timing, Jay-Jay. *(He looks around)* You got my coffee and doughnut?

ARTY   Oh. I forgot to tell him.

LOUIE   So tell him.

ARTY *(To JAY)*   Uncle Louie wanted some coffee and a doughnut.

JAY   Coming right up . . . Would you tell Grandma it's for you? Because doughnuts are expensive.

LOUIE *(Smiles)*   What is she doing, charging you for missing doughnuts?

JAY   No. Missing pretzels. How did you know?

LOUIE   It's her favorite trick. I once owed her two dollars for a missing bag of pistachio nuts. One minute they were on the counter, the next minute they were gone. She blamed me. Until I found them in her drawer. She said, "You're responsible if somebody steals from this store. Even me." . . . Hey, Arty. Get my shirt, will ya? It's on the bed.

(ARTY *crosses into* BELLA'*s room*)

JAY   Did you pay her the two dollars?

LOUIE   No. I stole the nuts back that night. But I got the lesson.

JAY   You've learned a lot in your life, haven't you, Uncle Louie?

LOUIE   No one takes me for pistachios no more.

(ARTY *comes out with* LOUIE*'s shirt*)

JAY   I can see . . . A guy could learn a lot from you, I bet.

LOUIE *(He takes the shirt and puts it on)*   I could write a book.

JAY   You wouldn't have to write. I mean, if someone just hung around you watching, they would pick up a lot, don't you think?

LOUIE *(He sits on the sofa and begins to shine his shoes)*   A lotta what?

JAY   A lot of anything.

LOUIE   I don't think so. 'Cause I don't like nobody hangin' around watchin' me.

JAY *(He looks at* ARTY, *then at* LOUIE)   Uncle Louie . . . I have an important question to ask you.

LOUIE   Don't ask questions, kid. That's probably the best thing I could teach you. Never ask questions.

JAY   I'm sorry . . . I'll just tell you then . . . I want to leave here . . . Tonight . . . I made up my mind. I'm definitely going . . .

LOUIE   Where you goin'?

JAY   As far away as I can get.

LOUIE How far away is that? Five-dollars far? Ten-dollars far? A dozen pretzels far?

JAY No. Just a-pair-of-shoes far. Until they wear out.

LOUIE And then what? You better have better transportation than a pair of shoes.

JAY I never did this before. That's why I'm asking your advice.

LOUIE You're gonna make your grandma very unhappy, Jay-Jay.

JAY No, I won't. Besides, that never stopped you.

(LOUIE *stops brushing and looks at* JAY)

ARTY Would you like me to brush your shoes, Uncle Louie?

LOUIE *(To* ARTY*)* Hey! One guy work on me at a time, okay? *(He brushes again; to* JAY*)* So why you wanna go? It's cold out there. It's lonely out there . . . and it's dangerous out there.

JAY I know that . . . but there's money out there.

LOUIE Oh, I see . . . You lookin' to get rich fast?

JAY Not for me. For Pop.

LOUIE Ain't that nice? Like Robin Hood, heh?

JAY I don't want to rob people.

LOUIE   No? . . . Who *do* you want to rob?

JAY   No one.

LOUIE   That sorta rules out gettin' rich fast.

JAY   *Some* people do it.

LOUIE   Yeah? How?

JAY   You'll think this is a question.

LOUIE *(Angrily)*   Then don't ask it. I can't help you, kid.
I got nothin' to teach you and nothin' I *wanna* teach
you . . . Is that what you think I do? Rob banks? Rob
liquor stores? Grocery stores? Little old ladies in the
park? Is that what you think I am?

JAY   No . . . I don't think so.

LOUIE   You don't think so? What is that, a compliment?
. . . You wanna know what I do? I'm a businessman.
I'm a free-lance money manager. A twenty-four-hour-
a-day investment adviser. You been dyin' to ask me that
all day so now I told you. School's out. You graduated.
Now find a girl and go to your prom, okay?

JAY   Thank you . . . I just have one minor question to ask.

LOUIE *(Smiles)*   You got balls, kid . . . Did you know you
got balls?

JAY   I'm aware of them, yes.

LOUIE *(To* ARTY*)*   I love your brother ... Reminds me
of me. *(To* JAY*)* What's your minor question?

JAY   Are there any openings in your business?

LOUIE *(Staring at him)*   ... You got balls but I think
they're in your head.

JAY   I'll do anything and I won't ask any questions.

LOUIE   There are no openings. The reason there are no
openings is because there's no business no more. I'm
relocating. I have urgent opportunities in a more desir-
able and advantageous territory. It's a one-man operation outa town ... That's the end of this conversation.
As far as I'm concerned, this conversation is deceased.
Okay?

JAY   ... Take me with you ... I'll get off wherever you
want me to, but please, take me with you tonight.

LOUIE   Are you deaf or somethin'? *(To* ARTY*)* Is he deaf?
Doesn't he hear what I just said? Did *you* hear what I
just said?

ARTY   I caught most of it, yeah.

LOUIE *(To* JAY*)*   Take you with me for what? For com-
pany? Your company's starting to pester me already.
What do I need you for? What can you do for me?
Heh?

   (He exits into the bathroom)

JAY   ... I could carry your little black satchel.

84

(LOUIE *comes out, wearing his shoulder holster. He* *has fire in his eyes.* LOUIE *moves toward* JAY)

LOUIE . . . You interested in my little black satchel?

JAY No . . . I just thought—

LOUIE No? But you want to carry it . . . Why? Does it look heavy to you? . . . You think I got a broken arm, I can't carry a little bag like that?

JAY No.

LOUIE So maybe you have some other interest in it . . . You been foolin' around with this bag?

JAY I swear. No.

LOUIE So what are you curious about? How much it weighs or something? . . . You want to pick it up, go ahead, pick it up.

JAY I don't want to pick it up.

LOUIE Pick it up, Jay. It ain't gonna bite you . . . You won't be happy till you pick it up. Go ahead, kid. Pick it up.

JAY I really don't want to.

ARTY Come on, Jay. Please pick it up.

JAY Stay out of this.

LOUIE No, no . . . Arty, come here.

ARTY Me?

LOUIE That's right. You're Arty. (ARTY *comes to him.*
LOUIE *puts his arm around* ARTY's *shoulder*) I want you
to go over to that stool and pick up the black bag.

ARTY Jay is closer.

LOUIE Jay is not interested. I want you to do it.

    (ARTY *goes over and stands next to the stool where the
black bag sits*) Okay, Arty. Pick it up.

ARTY (*His face screws up*) I don't know why but I think
I'm going to cry.

LOUIE Just pick it up, Arty.

    (ARTY *picks it up*) Is it heavy?

ARTY No.

LOUIE Is it light?

ARTY No.

LOUIE So what is it?

ARTY . . . Medium.

LOUIE Okay, so it's medium . . . So what do you think
is in the bag? . . . Money? . . . Fives and tens and
twenties and hundreds all stuck together with rubber
bands? . . . WHAT?? . . . I said *WHAT!!!*

ARTY I don't know.

LOUIE You don't know . . . Well, then, maybe you'd
better look in the bag and see . . . Why don't you do
that, Arty? . . . Open the bag . . . Okay?

ARTY Please, Uncle Louie—

LOUIE *(He takes a step closer)* I'm only gonna ask you one
more time, Arty . . . because I'm runnin' out of patience
. . . Open—the bag!

> (ARTY *looks at him, helpless, terrified . . . and then
> suddenly)*

JAY Don't do it, Arty . . . Leave him alone, Uncle Louie!
You want the bag open, do it yourself. *(He takes the bag
from* ARTY *and tosses it at* LOUIE'*s feet)* Maybe you don't
rob banks or grocery stores or little old women. You're
worse than that. You're a bully. You pick on a couple
of kids. Your own nephews. You make fun of my father
because he cried and was afraid of Grandma. Well,
everyone in *Yonkers* is afraid of Grandma . . . And let
me tell you something about my father. At least he's
doing something in this war. He's sick and he's tired
but he's out there selling iron to make ships and tanks
and cannons. And I'm proud of him. What are *you*
doing? Hiding in your mother's apartment and scaring
little kids and acting like Humphrey Bogart. Well,
you're no Humphrey Bogart . . . And I'll tell you
something else—No. That's all.

> (LOUIE *has hardly blinked an eye. He shifts his body
> and takes one small step towards* JAY)

LOUIE *(Smiles)*　That was thrilling. That was beautiful. I had tears in my eyes, I swear to God . . . You got bigger balls than I thought, Jay. You got a couple of steel basketballs there . . . You know what you got, Jay? You got moxie.

JAY　What's moxie?

LOUIE　Tell him, Arty.

(ARTY *makes* LOUIE*'s gesture of what moxie is*)

ARTY *(To* JAY*)*　That's moxie.

LOUIE　Yeah . . . Your father's a lucky guy, let me tell you . . . That's why I don't think you should go with me, Jay. You take care of Arty here. And Momma and Bella. And maybe one day you'll be proud of your old Uncle Louie, too. *(He picks up the bag and puts it on the table)* And don't worry what was in the bag. It's just laundry. Dirty laundry, boys. That's all.

(*He crosses to the mirror to finish getting dressed as* GRANDMA *walks in*)

GRANDMA *(Sternly, to* JAY*)*　Are you a banker? Is dis your lunch hour? Well, dis is not a bank. Go down and help Bella close up da store . . . Artur, get your clothes on. Ve haff company tonight.

(ARTY *runs into the bathroom*)

LOUIE　I don't think I can stay, Ma.

GRANDMA   I didn't ask you to. Bella asked you. You'll stay. *(To* JAY*)* You haff something to say to me? No? Den get downstairs . . . Und you und I haff someting else to talk about later.

JAY   About what?

GRANDMA   About a jar of pistachio nuts dat are missing, dot's about what.

(JAY *looks at* LOUIE, *then goes.* LOUIE *puts on his suit coat and hat.* GRANDMA *looks at him. It's more of a scowl. She takes a few bills out of her pocket)*

GRANDMA   You're getting careless, Louie. You dropped money on my dresser this morning.

LOUIE   Louie's never careless, Ma. It's for you. I had a good week.

GRANDMA   A good week for you is a bad week for someone else . . . I don't want your profits, Louie.

LOUIE   It's just a hundred bucks. Happy Birthday, Ma. It's tomorrow, right?

GRANDMA *(She puts the money on the table)*   Don't pay me for being born. I've been paid enough.

LOUIE *(He picks up the money)*   Then take it for putting me up. You know how I hate hotels.

(He offers it to her)

GRANDMA *(Angrily)* I don't take from you!!! . . . Not what you haff to give . . . You were always the strongest one. The survivor . . . *Live*—at any cost I taught you, yes. But not when someone else has to pay the price . . . Keep your filthy money, Louie. *(She starts to go)*

LOUIE *(Smiles)* You're terrific, Ma. One hundred percent steel. Finest grade made. Eddie's out there lookin' for scrap iron and the chump doesn't know he's got a whole battleship right here . . . Nah. You can't get me down, Ma. I'm too tough. You taught me good. And whatever I've accomplished in this life, just remember—you're my partner. *(He blows her a ferocious kiss)*

Blackout

In the dark, we hear the voice of EDDIE *again.*

EDDIE *(Voice-over)* "Dear Momma . . . The boys tell me you're getting along fine with them. I told you they wouldn't be any trouble. Enclosed, I'm sending you twenty-five dollars to cover their food and Arty's medicine . . . Yakob tells me some kids have been stealing pretzels and pistachio nuts. It's amazing that hasn't stopped in almost thirty years . . . Love, Eddie."

(Later that night.

BELLA *and* JAY *are clearing the dining table of its remaining dishes and straightening out the chairs.*

GRANDMA *sits in her usual chair, wearing a sweater and crocheting or doing needlepoint.* LOUIE, *wearing his suit jacket, paces, looking like he's anxious to go.* AUNT GERT, *in her mid-to-late thirties, sits on the sofa. She holds a purse and her handkerchief, which she uses now and then to wipe her mouth.* ARTY *is in the kitchen, unseen, helping clean off the dishes)*

BELLA   Would anyone like more coffee? Momma? Gert?

(GRANDMA *doesn't answer*)

GERT *(Nods)*   Mmm.

BELLA   Strudel with it?

GERT *(Hoarsely)*   No.

BELLA Jay, go in and get Aunt Gert some more coffee, but no strudel. *(JAY goes in)* Louie? Wouldn't you like another piece?

LOUIE *(Distracted)* I had enough, Bella.

BELLA You always have two pieces.

LOUIE One strudel is enough tonight, okay, Bella?

> *(He looks at his watch . . .* BELLA *starts to put the chairs from the dining table into the circle of seats in the living room)*

BELLA Don't help me with the chairs, anyone. I know just how I want it to be.

> *(*LOUIE *looks at his watch as* BELLA *puts a chair in the right spot)*

LOUIE Listen, Momma. I'm gonna run along, now. I'll call you next week. Gert, it was good seein' you, sweetheart. You're lookin' terrific.

BELLA Louie, you're going to sit right here.

LOUIE Bella, I'm sorry. I really gotta go. It was a top-notch dinner, no kiddin'. *(He kisses her cheek. He calls off into the kitchen)* Jay! It'll work out. Trust me. Where's Arty? I'm leavin'.

BELLA Noo!! You can't go yet, Louie . . . You promised.

LOUIE I promised I'd stay for dinner. I stayed for dinner. How many dinners you want me to stay for?

BELLA   But the family hasn't had a talk yet.

LOUIE   We did. We talked all through dinner. I never had a chance to swallow nothin'. I'm all talked out, Bella.

BELLA   There's still something that hasn't been talked about. It wasn't something that could be talked about at dinner . . . You sit here. This is your place.

LOUIE *(Exasperated)*   I told you I had to go right after the coffee. I had my coffee. I had my strudel. I had my dinner. I have to go, Bella.

BELLA *(Nervously)*   Momma! Gert! Tell him to stay . . . Louie, you can't go. You have to be here. The whole family has to be here. Momma, tell him.

GRANDMA *(Sternly)*   You're getting excited, Bella.

BELLA   I won't get excited. I promise. I'm fine, Momma . . . Just ask Louie to stay. Let me get the boys in.

GERT   He'll stay, Bella.

BELLA *(Calls out)*   Jay? Arty! Forget the dishes. We'll do them later . . . Everybody inside.

> (JAY *comes in with* GERT's *coffee.* ARTY *follows, eating the last bite of a piece of strudel. He is dressed now)*

JAY   Here's your coffee, Aunt Gert.

GERT   Thank you.

BELLA   Jay! Arty! Sit on the sofa with Aunt Gert. Momma, you stay there. I'll sit here and, Louie, sit on the chair.

LOUIE   I've been sittin' all night, Bella. I can stand up, okay?

BELLA   But it would be so much better if you were sitting, Louie. I pictured everybody sitting.

LOUIE   *I don't wanna sit!!* Change the picture. Picture everybody sittin' and me standin', alright?

   (*This is the first time we hear* AUNT GERT *say her first full sentence, where her affliction becomes apparent. She speaks normally for the first half of the sentence and then somewhere past the middle, she sucks in her breath, so the words go to a higher pitch and it sounds very difficult for her*)

GERT   Louie, can't you just sit for a few minutes until Bella tells us what it is— (*She sucks in now*)—she wants to talk to us about.

   (ARTY *and* JAY *look at each other*)

LOUIE   Okay. Okay. (*He sits on the window seat*) Here? Alright? Is this the way you pictured it, Bella?

BELLA   No. I pictured you sitting on the chair I picked out.

LOUIE (*He crosses to "his" chair, but doesn't sit*)   Bella! It's *very* important that I leave here soon. Very important.

I don't want to upset you, sweetheart, but I can't spend the rest of the night getting the seating arrangements right . . . I'm gonna stand up, I'm gonna listen, and then I'm gonna go.

BELLA *(She puts her head down and sulks, childlike)*   I pictured everybody sitting.

LOUIE   Jesus!

GERT   Louie, stop arguing with her and sit down, for God sakes, before—*(She sucks in)*—she gets into one of her moods again.

GRANDMA   Louie, sit! Gertrude, stop it.

LOUIE   Louie sit! Louie stand! Louie eat! . . . You don't scare me anymore, Ma. Maybe everyone else here, but not me. You understand?

GRANDMA *(Still crocheting)*   Sit down, Louie!

(LOUIE *sits)*

BELLA   Alright. *(She sits)* Are we all seated now?

LOUIE   Yes, Bella. We're all seated. You wanna take a picture of what you pictured?

GERT   Stop it, Louie.

BELLA *(She looks around, then smiles, content with the seating)*   Now . . . who wants to start?

LOUIE *(Rises)* Who wants to *start?* . . . Start *what?* . . . Momma, I haven't got time for this. Maybe when I was twelve years old, but not tonight. It's one of her games. Her crazy games, for crise sakes.

GERT Is this a game, Bella? Are you just playing— *(Sucks in)*—a game with us, darling?

BELLA It's not a game. It's very important . . . But I don't know how to start to say it. So somebody else has to help me and start first.

LOUIE *(To* BELLA*)* You have something important to tell us and you want *us* to start? *(He starts toward the front door)* Listen, Gert. You understand her better than I do. When you figure out what it is, let me know.

JAY *(To* BELLA*)* Aunt Bella, have you . . . *(*LOUIE *and everyone else stop and look at* JAY*)* . . . Have you been going to the movies lately, Aunt Bella?

BELLA *(She smiles)* Thank you, Jay . . . Yes. I have been going to the movies a lot lately . . . *(*LOUIE *looks at her in disbelief)* . . . Three times last week.

JAY Really? . . . Did you see anything good?

BELLA Oh, yes. I saw a picture with William Holden and Jean Arthur . . . I really liked it . . . That's why I saw it three times.

LOUIE This is what I stayed to dinner for? This is what I had to sit in the right seat to listen to? Jean Arthur and William Holden? Are they in the picture you pictured here?

GERT   Is that what this is about, Bella? Is this all about what movies—*(Sucks in)*—you went to last week?

BELLA   No, but I'm getting to it. Ask me more questions, Jay. You're good at this.

JAY   Uh, let's see . . . Did you—go alone?

BELLA   Oh, yes. I always go alone. But it's interesting you asked me that . . . Because I met a friend there . . . You can ask me questions too, Gert.

GERT   I don't know what kind of questions—*(Sucks in)*—to ask you.

ARTY   Ask her who the friend was.

GERT   Who was the friend?

BELLA   Well, his name is Johnny, I always see him there because he's the head usher. He's very nice.

JAY   So you just saw him in the theater?

BELLA   Well, once or twice we went out for coffee and once we took a walk in the park.

LOUIE   . . . You went to the park with this guy?

BELLA   Just to talk . . . You have to sit down if you're going to ask me questions, Louie. *(LOUIE comes back and sits down)* Now whose turn is it?

GRANDMA   Dis is ven you came home at eleven o'clock?

BELLA   Maybe. I think so. Was that it?

GERT   What did you do until eleven—*(Sucks in)*—o'clock?

BELLA   We walked and we talked . . . And we got to know each other . . . He doesn't want to be an usher forever. One day he wants to open up his own restaurant.

LOUIE   His own restaurant? And he's an usher? What is he, fifteen, sixteen?

BELLA   No. He's forty . . . And he wants to open up the restaurant with me.

(*There is silence. She has finally gotten their attention*)

LOUIE   Why with you?

BELLA *(Starting to get nervous)*   Because I can do all the cooking . . . and write out the menus . . . and keep the books.

GERT   And what would he do?

BELLA   He would be the manager.

(*She sees this isn't going too well*)

LOUIE   If he's the manager, why doesn't *he* write out the menus and keep the books?

BELLA   Well, he has a—*(She looks at* ARTY *and* JAY*)*—a reading handicap.

LOUIE   A what?

BELLA   A reading handicap.

LOUIE   Okay, hold it. Wait a minute. *(He rises)* What do you mean? He can't read?

BELLA   You're not supposed to get out of your chair. That's not how I pictured it.

LOUIE   Yeah, well, now I'm getting my *own* picture . . . This guy is what? Illiterate?

BELLA   He can read . . . a little.

LOUIE   What's a little? His *name?* . . . This guy is either pulling your leg or he's after something, Bella . . . Is he after something?

BELLA   Maybe this isn't a good time to talk about it.

LOUIE   No, it's the *perfect* time to talk about it . . . What is this guy after, Bella? Has he touched you? . . . Has he fooled around with you?

BELLA   NO!!! He's not that kind of person.

LOUIE   Well, what kinda person *is* he? . . . He's forty years old, he takes you to the park at night. He wants to open up a restaurant with you and he can't read or write . . . How are you going to open up a restaurant? Who's going to put up the money?

BELLA   It'll only cost five thousand dollars.

LOUIE   *(Laughs)*   Five thousand dollars? Why not five million? And who's got the five grand? Him?

BELLA   I don't think so . . . He doesn't have any money.

LOUIE   Oh. Too bad . . . Well, then who does that leave?

BELLA   Don't yell at me, Louie.

LOUIE   I'm not yelling at you, Bella. I'm just asking you a question. Who does that leave to put up the five thousand dollars?

GERT   This is too terrible. Momma, please tell them— *(Sucks in)*—to stop this awful thing.

LOUIE   Who does that leave, Bella?

BELLA   I'll get the money somewhere.

LOUIE   Where is somewhere, Bella? . . . There is no somewhere. You want Momma to sell the store? Is that what this guy asked you to do?

BELLA   He didn't ask me anything.

LOUIE   And he's either very smart or very dangerous. Well, he doesn't sound too smart to me. So that just leaves dangerous.

BELLA   He's *not* dangerous.

LOUIE   How do you know that?

BELLA   Because they don't take you at the Home if you're dangerous.

LOUIE   . . . The *Home???*

GRANDMA   Oh, my Gott!!

GERT   I don't understand this. Can somebody please— *(She sucks in)*—explain all this to me.

LOUIE *(To* BELLA*)*   Bella, honey. This man sounds very troubled . . . Is he living at the Home now?

BELLA   No. With his parents. He didn't like the Home. They weren't very nice to him there. *(She looks at* GRANDMA, *pointedly)* . . . It's *not a nice place*, Momma!

LOUIE   Bella, sweetheart. Don't go to that movie anymore. Don't see that fella again. He may be very nice but he sounds like he's got a lot of whacky ideas, you know what I mean, sweetheart?

BELLA   You promised you would support me . . . Jay! Arty! You said you would back me up. You promised.

LOUIE   Back you up with what, Bella? . . . The restaurant? The money? Is that what this guy is after?

BELLA   He wants *more* than that.

LOUIE   What could possibly be more than that, Bella?

BELLA   Me! He wants *me!* He wants to marry me! *(She starts to cry)* I want to marry *him* . . . I want to have his children . . . I want my own babies.

LOUIE *(Sits back)*   Jesus Christ!

GRANDMA *(Shocked at this)*   Dot's enough! . . . I don't vant to hear dis anymore!

BELLA   You think I can't have healthy babies, Momma? Well, I can . . . I'm as strong as an ox. I've worked in that store and taken care of you by myself since I'm twelve years old, that's how strong I am . . . Like *steel*, Momma. Isn't that how we're supposed to be? . . . But my babies won't die because I'll love them and take care of them . . . And they won't get sick like me or Gert or be weak like Eddie and Louie . . . My babies will be happier than we were because I'll teach them to be happy . . . Not to grow up and run away or never visit when they're older or not be able to breathe because they're so frightened . . . and never, *ever* to make them spend their lives rubbing my back and my legs because you never had anyone around who loved you enough to want to touch you because you made it so clear you never wanted to be touched with love . . . Do you know what it's like to touch steel, Momma? It's hard and it's cold and I want to be warm and soft with my children . . . Let me have my babies, Momma. Because I have to love somebody. I have to love someone who'll love me back before I die . . . Give me that, Momma, and I promise you, you'll never worry about being alone . . . Because you'll have us . . . Me and my husband and my babies . . . Louie, tell her how wonderful that would be . . . Gert, wouldn't that make her happy? . . . Momma? . . . Please say yes . . . I need you to say yes . . . Please?

(It is deathly silent. No one has moved. Finally, GRANDMA *gets up slowly, walks to her room, goes in, and quietly closes the door.*

BELLA *looks at the others)*

Hold me . . . Somebody please hold me.

*(*GERT *gets up and puts her arms around* BELLA *and rocks her gently.*

We go to black)

ARTY *(Voice-over)* "Dear Pop . . . Things are really bad here. Really, *really* bad. I wish you were home. Even just for a weekend. Last night I cried for you . . . and for Mom . . . but Jay was afraid Grandma would hear, so he stuck a sock in my mouth. I miss you and love you. Your son, Arty . . . Not Artur."

(Sunday, the following week. About midday.

ARTY is seated at the table, writing in his notebook. JAY stands looking out the window)

JAY   Where do you think Aunt Bella could be? Missing for two nights, somewhere out there in the city. I'm worried.

ARTY   Maybe Uncle Louie took her with him.

JAY   If he didn't take me, you think he's going to take Aunt Bella and her forty-year-old usher from the Home? . . .

(The door to GRANDMA's room opens and AUNT GERT comes out)

GERT   I'm going now. I think Momma feels better since—*(A breath)*—Aunt Bella called me.

JAY   No idea where she is?

GERT   Yes. *(She moves away from GRANDMA's door)* . . . She's at my house.

JAY   *Your* house?

GERT   Shhh. She doesn't want Momma to know.

ARTY   You mean she's been there all the time?

(GERT *nods "yes"*)

JAY   Is she ever coming back?

GERT   She's meeting with that man today ... We'll know soon.

ARTY   Do you think they'll get married?

GERT   Who knows? . . . She's been crying for—*(A breath)*—two days now. I'm sorry. It's hard for me to talk.

JAY   Isn't there anything the doctors can do about that, Aunt Gert?

GERT   I don't have it that much. It's mostly—*(Sucks in)*—when I come here.

JAY   Oh.

GERT   You boys take care of Grandma now. If Bella doesn't come back you're all she has.

JAY   I know.

GERT   If you run into trouble, do you have my number?

JAY   I don't think so.

GERT It's Westchester seven—*(Sucks in)*—four-six-six-nine.

ARTY What?

GERT Westchester seven—*(Sucks in)*—four-six—

JAY I have it! I have it!

GERT Goodbye, darlings. Take care. I love you. *(She goes, closing the front door)*

ARTY It could be worse. Suppose we were left with *her* instead?

JAY That's not funny.

ARTY Yes, it is.

JAY Alright. It's funny. But I feel sorry for her. I feel sorry for this whole family . . . Even Grandma . . . Don't you? *(*ARTY *looks at* JAY, *says nothing)* Well, I do. And you should, too. *(*GRANDMA*'s door opens. She comes out, looking tired)* Hi, Grandma. How you feeling?

ARTY Is there anything we can get you?

GRANDMA *(She sits)* Vot are you doing in the house on Sunday? Vy don't you go for a walk or something?

JAY We thought we'd keep you company.

GRANDMA I don't need to be kept company.

ARTY You want the radio on, Grandma? They have Sunday news on today.

GRANDMA I had enough news already this week.

JAY Things are getting better in North Africa. They captured twenty thousand Germans this month.

GRANDMA Twenty thousand Germans . . . Goot. Dot's goot news.

ARTY The football game is on now. Sometimes they interrupt the game for news reports.

GRANDMA Don't trick me into listening to football. *(She turns her head)* Vas dot the phone? Did you hear the phone downstairs?

JAY No.

GRANDMA No. It don't ring on Sundays . . . How is your father?

JAY He's feeling better. He thinks he could be home for good in about eight months.

GRANDMA Eight months . . . You'll be glad to go home, ya?

ARTY Ya . . . Yes . . . Sort of.

JAY But we'll still come out and visit you, Grandma.

GRANDMA Maybe I von't be here . . . Maybe I'll sell da store.

JAY   Sell the store? What would you do without the store?

GRANDMA   Don't worry so much about your grandma. Your grandma knows how to take care of herself, believe me . . . Go on outside, both of you. You talk too much.

JAY   You sure you don't mind being alone?

GRANDMA *(She sits back and closes her eyes)*   . . . Maybe dis is da first Sunday I'll get some rest.

(The front door opens and BELLA *comes in. She is wearing a hat and coat and carries her purse and a small suitcase. She also has a cake box)*

JAY   Aunt Bella!

ARTY   Are you okay?

GRANDMA *(She doesn't react to this. She remains sitting back with her eyes still closed)*   Go already. How many times do I haff to tell you?

(The boys look at her, then turn and leave, closing the door. BELLA *stands there looking at her mother, who has still refused to open her eyes)*

BELLA   Hello, Momma . . . (GRANDMA *doesn't respond)* . . . Would you like some tea? It's chilly in here . . . I bought a coffee cake at Grossman's. It's still warm . . . It's alright if you don't want to talk to me, Momma. I know you must be very angry with me.

GRANDMA *(She looks away from* BELLA*)*   You're home for goot or dis is a visit?

BELLA   I don't know . . . I thought I'd come back and talk to you about it.

GRANDMA   Like you talked to me da night you left? . . . Vidout a vord?

BELLA   You're the one who didn't talk, Momma. You never gave me a chance to say anything.

GRANDMA   I heard vot you had to say. I didn't haff to hear no more.

BELLA *(Nods)*   Look, Momma, I'm not crying . . . I know you're very angry with me but I'm not crying. And it's not because I'm afraid to cry. It's because I have no tears left in me. I feel sort of empty inside. Like *you* feel all the time.

GRANDMA   How vould you know how I feel?

BELLA   You don't think I know anything, do you? You think I'm stupid, don't you, Momma?

GRANDMA   No. You're not stupid.

BELLA   Then what? Am I crazy? Do you think I'm crazy, Momma?

GRANDMA   Don't use dot word to me.

BELLA   Why not? Are you afraid of it? If that's what I am, Momma, then don't be afraid to say it. Because if

I'm crazy, I should be in the Home, shouldn't I? But then you'd be alone and you wouldn't like that. Is that why you don't use that word, Momma?

GRANDMA . . . You vant to know vot you are, Bella? . . . You're a child. Dot's vot da doctors told me. Not crazy. Not stupid . . . A child! . . . And dot's how I treat you. Because dot's all you understand . . . You don't need doctors. You're not sick. You don't need to live in da Home. *Dis* is vere you live. Vere you can be vatched and taken care of . . . You'll always be a child, Bella. And in dis vorld, vere dere is so much hate and sickness and death, vere nobody can live in peace, den maybe you're better off . . . Stay a child, Bella, and be glad dot's vot Gott made you.

BELLA Then why did he make me look like a woman? . . . And feel like a woman inside of me? And want all the things a woman should have? Is that what I should thank him for? Why did he do that, Momma, when I can do everything but *think* like a woman? . . . I know I get confused sometimes . . . and frightened. But if I'm a child, why can't I be happy like a child? Why can't I be satisfied with dolls instead of babies?

GRANDMA I'm not so smart I can answer such things.

BELLA But I *am* smart, Momma. Maybe only as smart as a child, but some children are smarter than grown-ups. Some grown-ups I've seen are very stupid. And very mean.

GRANDMA You don't haff responsibilities, Bella. And responsibilities is vot makes meanness.

BELLA   I don't want to be your responsibility. Then maybe you won't be so mean to me.

GRANDMA   Den who will be responsible for you? Yourself? Dot man you ran away with? Who vants money from you? Who wants other things from you? God only knows vot else. Things you vould never know about. Stay the way you are, Bella, because you don't know vot such feelings vould do to you.

BELLA   Yes, I do, Momma. I know what other things you're talking about . . . Because they've happened to me, Momma . . . Oh, yes . . . They've happened because I *wanted* them to happen . . . You angry at me?

GRANDMA   *(She turns away, dismissing this)*   You don't know vot you're saying, Bella.

BELLA   You mean am I telling you the truth? Yes. I know what the truth is . . . Only I've been afraid to tell it to you for all these years. Gertrude knows. She's the only one . . . Do you hate me, Momma? Tell me, because I don't know if I did wrong or not.

GRANDMA   You're angry so you tell me lies. I don't vant to hear your childish lies.

   (She waves BELLA away)

BELLA   No! You *have* to listen, Momma . . . When I was in school, I let boys touch me . . . And boys that I met in the park . . . And in the movies . . . Even boys that I met here in the store . . . Nights when you were asleep, I went down and let them in . . . And not just boys, Momma . . . men too.

GRANDMA   Stop dis, Bella. You don't know vot you're saying . . . You dream these things in your head.

BELLA   I needed somebody to touch me, Momma. Somebody to hold me. To tell me I was pretty . . . *You* never told me that. Some even told me they loved me but I never believed them because I knew what they wanted from me . . . Except John. He *did* love me. Because he understood me. Because he was like me. He was the only one I ever felt safe with. And I thought maybe for the first time I *could* be happy . . . That's why I ran away. I even brought the five thousand dollars to give to him for the restaurant. Then maybe he'd find the courage to leave home too.

GRANDMA *(She looks at her disdainfully)*   Is dis someting else you dreamed up? Vere vould you get five thousand dollars?

    (BELLA *opens her purse and takes out a stack of bills tied in rubber bands. She puts it on the table)*

BELLA   Does this look like a dream, Momma?

GRANDMA *(She picks up the bills and looks at them)*   Vere did you get dis? *(She turns quickly and looks toward her room)* Did you steal from me? You know vere I keep my money. Nobody else knows but you. *(She throws her cup of tea in* BELLA*'s face)* You thief!! You steal from your own mother? *Thief!!*

BELLA *(Screams at her)*   Go on, hit me, Momma! Crack my head open, make me stupid and crazy, because that's what you really think anyway, isn't it?

GRANDMA   Get out of my house. Go live vith your thief friend. You vant da rest of the money, go, take it . . . It von't last you long . . . You'll both haff to steal again to keep alive, believe me.

BELLA   I don't want the rest of your money . . . You can have this too . . . Louie gave it to me. I stayed in Gertrude's house the last two nights . . . Louie came to say goodbye and he gave me this out of his little black satchel and God knows how much more he had . . . I didn't ask him. Maybe he's a thief too, Momma, but he's my brother and he loved me enough to want to help me . . . Thieves and sick little girls, that's what you have, Momma . . . Only God didn't make them that way. *You* did. We're alive, Momma, but that's all we are . . . Aaron and Rose are the lucky ones.

GRANDMA *(Crushed)*   NOOO!! . . . Don't say dat! . . . Please Gott, don't say dat to me, Bella.

BELLA   I'm sorry, Momma . . . I didn't mean to hurt you.

GRANDMA   Yes. You do . . . It's my punishment for being alive . . . for surviving my own children . . . Not dying before them is my sin . . . Go, Bella. Take Louie's money . . . You tink I don't know vot he is . . . He stole since he vas five years old . . . The year Aaron died . . . And I closed off from him and everybody . . . From you and Louie . . . From Gert and Eddie . . . I lost Rose, then Aaron, and I stopped feeling because I couldn't stand losing anymore . . .

BELLA   Momma!

GRANDMA   Go open your restaurant, live your own life, haff your own babies. If it's a mistake, let it be your mistake . . . If I've done wrong by you, then it's for me to deal with . . . That's how I've lived my life and no one, not even you, can change that for me now.

BELLA   . . . There is no restaurant, Momma . . . He's afraid to be a businessman or a manager . . . He likes being an usher . . . He likes to be in the dark all day, watching movies whenever he wants . . . Then he can live in a world he can feel safe in . . . He doesn't want babies . . . He doesn't want to get married . . . He wants to live with his parents because he knows that they love him . . . And that's enough for him.

GRANDMA   Then maybe he's more lucky than you.

BELLA   Maybe he is . . . But I'll never stop wanting what I don't have . . . It's too late to go back for me . . . Maybe I'm still a child but now there's just enough woman in me to make me miserable. We have to learn how to deal with that somehow, you and me . . . And it can never be the same anymore . . . *(She gets up)* I'll put my things away . . . I think we've both said enough for today . . . don't you?

(BELLA *picks up her things, crosses into her room, and closes the door.*

GRANDMA *sits, stoically . . . and then her hand goes to her mouth, stifling whatever feelings are beginning to overcome her.*

(We go to black)

BELLA *(Voice-over)* "Dear Eddie . . . This postcard is from Bella. I just want to tell you that Arty and Jay are alright and I have good news for you except I don't have no more room. Love, Bella."

(Nine months later. We hear the church bells chime.

ARTY and JAY are dressed in the same outfits they wore on that first day. They each have a suitcase sitting in the middle of the room)

ARTY   . . . How long you think Pop's going to be in there?

JAY   I don't know, but we made it, Arty. Ten months here and we're still alive. We got through Grandma and we're alright.

ARTY   You know who I miss? Uncle Louie . . . I'm glad those two guys never caught him.

JAY   No, but maybe the Japs will. You think he's safer fighting in the South Pacific?

ARTY   No. But he's probably the richest guy on Guadalcanal.

(The front door opens and BELLA comes in carrying two shopping bags)

BELLA   Oh, thank God. I thought you'd be gone before I got back. I ran all over Yonkers looking for these

. . . *(She puts the bags down)* Okay. Close your eyes. *(They do. She takes out a basketball and a football. She gives the basketball to* JAY*)* The football is for you, Jay. *(She gives the football to* ARTY*)* And the basketball is for you, Arty. Do you like 'em?

ARTY   Ho-lee mackerel!

JAY   This is incredible.

BELLA   I hope it's the right size. I just took a guess.

JAY   This is one of the best gifts I ever got, Aunt Bella.

BELLA   Well, you two were the best gifts I ever got too. I hate to give you up.

JAY   You don't have to. We're coming out all the time.

ARTY   I really love this, Aunt Bella. Thank you.

BELLA   Well, it's not just from me. It's from Grandma too. I just have to tell her later.

(The bedroom door opens and EDDIE *comes out)*

EDDIE   Well, Grandma and I are through talking, boys. You ready to go?

JAY   Hey, Pop. Look! It's from Aunt Bella. And Grandma.

ARTY   Aunt Bella, go out for a pass.

(GRANDMA *comes out of the bedroom, just as* ARTY
throws the football to JAY)

GRANDMA   Vot's dis? Vot did I tell you about games in
da house?

EDDIE   They're not playing games, Momma. They know
better than that.

GRANDMA   If dey break someting, dey'll pay plenty, believe me.

JAY   Thank you for the ball, Grandma. I love it.

ARTY   I never owned a football in my life, Grandma.

EDDIE   Alright. Grandma's tired, boys. Let's say goodbye and go.

GRANDMA   Ve said goodbye dis morning. Two goodbyes
is too much.

EDDIE   *(With some sincerity)*   Well, Momma . . . I just
wanted to say thank you. You did a lot for me and the
boys. I don't know how to repay you for that.

GRANDMA   I'll tell you how. Don't do it again.

EDDIE   I pray to God I won't have to.

GRANDMA   And if you have to, I'll say no again. And this
time I'll mean it . . . When Louie left for the army, I
thought about sending you the money. Even Bella
asked me to. But then I said no . . . Eddie has to do
things for himself. And you did it. That's good.

EDDIE   Yes, Momma. I'm glad you finally approve of me.

GRANDMA   I didn't say that. All I said was "Good."

EDDIE   I'll accept that, Momma.

GRANDMA   So, I suppose you'll get married again, and I won't see your boys for another ten years.

EDDIE   I'm not ready for marriage yet, Momma, but from now on the boys won't be strangers anymore. They'll be grandchildren . . . And I'm going to kiss you good-bye whether you like it or not. *(He leans over and kisses her)* Thank you for not putting up a fight. *(He nods, then turns to* BELLA*)* Goodbye, Bella. What can I say?

BELLA   I know, Eddie. I know.

EDDIE   I love you so much. *(He hugs her)* I'll meet you downstairs, boys. Thank Grandma, go on.

(And he goes before the tears come)

JAY   I er . . . I just want to say thank you for taking us in, Grandma. I know it wasn't easy for you.

GRANDMA   Dot's right. It vasn't.

JAY   It wasn't easy for us either. But I think I learned a lot since I'm here. Some good and some bad. Do you know what I mean, Grandma?

GRANDMA   *(She looks up at him)*   You're not afraid to say the truth. Dot's good . . . You want to hear what my truth is? . . . Everything hurts. Whatever it is you get good in life, you also lose someting.

JAY I guess I'm too young to understand that.

GRANDMA And I'm too old to forget it . . . Go on. Go home. Take care of your father. He's a good boy but he always needs a little help.

(JAY *nods and crosses to the door, waiting for* ARTY)

ARTY Well, you sure gave me and Yakob a lot of help, Grandma. Danker Schein . . . That means, "Thank you."

GRANDMA He's sneaky, dis one. Tries to get around me . . . Don't try to change me. Sometimes old people aren't altogether wrong.

ARTY You're absolutely right . . . Can King Artur give you a kiss goodbye?

(*He kisses her and crosses to the door*)

GRANDMA . . . What were you two looking for that night under the boysenberry? My money maybe?

ARTY No! I swear!

GRANDMA You should have looked behind the malted machine.

(*The boys hit themselves for their stupidity and leave.* BELLA *looks at her mother*)

BELLA   Well, I'll get dinner started . . . Do you mind eating early, because I'm going out tonight. With a friend. (GRANDMA *looks at her*) It's a girl, Momma. I have a new girlfriend. She likes me and I like her . . . And she also has a brother I like . . . He works in the library . . . He can read everything . . . I'd like to have them both over for dinner one night . . . Can we do that, Momma? (GRANDMA *looks away, not knowing how to deal with this*) It's alright . . . It's no rush. You don't have to make up your mind right now. *(She turns on the radio)* . . . I thought Thursday would be a good night. *(The music, "Be Careful, It's My Heart" sung by Bing Crosby, comes up.* BELLA *hums along happily)* It's called music, Momma.

(And she disappears into the kitchen.

GRANDMA *watches* BELLA, *then nods her head as if to say, "So it's come to this . . .")*

Curtain